COWBOY

SPUR MAKER

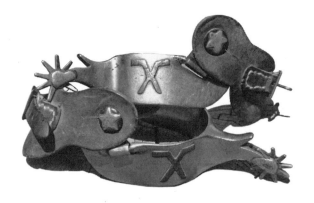

Cowboy Spur Maker

THE STORY OF ED BLANCHARD

Jane Pattie & Tom Kelly

TEXAS A&M UNIVERSITY PRESS   COLLEGE STATION

The paper used in this book meets the minimum requirements
of the American National Standard for Permanence
of Paper for Printed Library Materials, z39.48-1984.
Binding materials have been chosen for durability.

Afterword adapted from "Then and Now" by Tom Kelly, from *Celebrating 100
Years of Frontier Living*, published by Magdalena Old Timers Association, 1994,
with their permission.

Library of Congress Cataloging-in-Publication Data

Pattie, Jane, 1935–
    Cowboy spur maker : the story of Ed Balanchard / Jane Pattie and
Tom Kelly.
        p. cm.
    Includes bibliographical references and index.
    ISBN 1-58544-174-0 (cloth)
    1. Blanchard, Edward Fred, 1894–1982.   2. Blacksmiths—New Mexico—
Biography.   3. Ranchers—New Mexico—Biography.   4. Spurs—New
Mexico.   I. Title: Story of Ed Blanchard.   II. Kelly, Tom, 1925–   III. Title.
TT220.P39   2002
682'.092—dc21   2001006542

CONTENTS

ILLUSTRATIONS

MUCHAS GRACIAS

This is the story of Ed Blanchard, but it is also the story of the people and times and the country that molded him. It is a story that has come together with the help of many of Ed's family and friends as well as the users and collectors of Blanchard bits and spurs. We give our thanks to them for both their time and their generosity in sharing their knowledge, photos, and spurs. All have added to this story of the noted cowboy spur maker and the times that molded him.

A. C. "Ace" Cook, living in New Mexico but a resident of Denton, Texas, when I first met him in 1994, had a pair of early-day Blanchard spurs that were made for a cowman named Tipton who ranched near Luna, New Mexico. I first saw and admired them at the annual Bit and Spur Show in Abilene, Texas. They were nothing like the more familiar, sleek, modernistic Blanchard styles of later years. Since I was interested in Blanchard's early spurs, Ace suggested that I contact Mary K. and Dale Gallaher of Magdalena, New Mexico, who also had a pair of Blanchard spurs of a similar vintage.

I made a trip to Magdalena, and through the Gallahers, I met rancher Tom Kelly of Water Canyon, a cousin of Ed Blanchard's. The result was our collaboration on this book. Without Tom Kelly and his personal knowledge and contacts and his cowboy way of spinning a yarn, this book would never have come about. My thanks to Tom for his photos and tales of Water Canyon and the intertwined family of Blanchard/Tinguely/Kelly. I will always remember the fun we had making tracks on and around Mount Baldy and across Blanchard country. A special thanks to both Tom and Hilda Kelly for their hospitality and time away from busy days.

Much credit for this book goes to William "Billy" Cook of Sparks, Nevada, who grew up around Ed Blanchard and was close to him until Ed's death. It was Billy Cook who recalled the stories of Ed's years at the Currycomb Ranch in New Mexico as well as his later years in Arizona.

Tom joins me in thanking the Rueben Pankeys of Santa Fe, New Mexico, who made their family spur collection available for photographing. They have George Latham's spurs, some of the first Ed built. Thanks also go to the Clay Hendersons for making available Drew Henderson's spurs and bit and to Bern Henderson for allowing us to photograph his Blanchard spurs. Thanks to Felix Martinez of southern New Mexico, who shared his Hugh Pankey spurs. It was Hugh Pankey who gave Ed Blanchard his first lessons in spur making at the original Rueben Pankey ranch north of Monticello, New Mexico. We also photographed the spurs of Ira Sullivan, Eddie Henderson, Fred Martin, Frank Tucker, and Pete Segulia. And thanks also go to Bill Swope of Cherokee, Texas, whose spur collection includes two outstanding pairs of Ed's workmanship.

We are also indebted to Blanchard kinfolk—one of Ed's nieces, Linda Blanchard Whitaker of Clovis, New Mexico, and a nephew, Richard Prince of Saint Joseph, Missouri, and Prince's daughter, Judy Boyce of Bullard, Texas. Thanks also go to Suzanne Smith Dean of Socorro, New Mexico, for use of the outstanding photos from her J. E. Smith Collection of early-day scenes of the Socorro-Magdalena area.

Our thanks also to Blanchard afficionado Mel Gnatkowski of Carrizozo, New Mexico, for allowing us to use his images of Ed's spurs. Mel is not only a fine photographer, but he also hammers out spurs in the Blanchard tradition.

Tom and I hope that this book of tales about Ed Blanchard country adds meaning to the jingling spurs on your boot heels, especially if they are stamped E.F.B. inside the heel bands. Ol' Ed would like that.

Part I

Ed Blanchard Country

CHAPTER 1

As I Know the Story

by Jane Pattie

The stout two-year-old maverick bull stirred up the dust as he charged down the steep mountainside above a wide canyon in New Mexico's San Mateo Mountains. Hot on his heels rode a wild and reckless cowboy, rope in hand and swinging a big loop. Just as the bull headed for escape down the canyon's rock slide, the cowboy let his loop fly. He reached way out and caught the animal by a front foot. The bull turned a flip and somersaulted out through space, picking up momentum on its downhill flight. Ed Blanchard had secured the rope's horn loop to his saddle, and when the bovine hit the end of the rope, it jerked the horse and rider along, too. As the bull shot past a big tree, the cowboy and his horse catapulted by the tree on the opposite side. The horse's fall momentarily slowed as the rope caught and stretched taut. It snapped, and man and animals bounced on down the rocks. It was a terrible wreck. When the cowboy finally rolled to a stop, he just sat there and shook his head. That had been some ride! Ed was always an accident looking for a place to happen.

Ed Blanchard's family and friends in central New Mexico knew him as a wild, reckless cowboy long before horsemen of the West recognized him as a noted maker of cowboy spurs. His years of herding snorty cattle and cinching his saddle on broncs in the Magdalena and San Mateo Mountains near Socorro had taught him his trade as a cowboy and a spur maker.

Blanchard made spurs that fit a cowboy's boots. He knew his business because he was a cowboy before he became a spur maker. He was a product of the cattle country. The harsh land and the hard men he knew and worked alongside molded him, as did the wild cattle he hunted and the tough horses he rode. He was the son of strong, adventurous pioneers. He was one of the interwoven family of Tinguelys, Blanchards, and Kellys who put down a long taproot in Water Canyon, a slash in the shoulder of central New Mexico's Mount Baldy.

From the top of Mount Baldy, Ed Blanchard could survey his universe: east past Socorro to the Rio Grande as it cut a brown swath southward through the state toward Mexico, northeastward across the Flat toward the old Spanish town of Albuquerque, and southwest through the land of the Apaches, of Geronimo, Mangas Coloradas, and Victorio. He could look down the Alamosa River toward the Currycomb Ranch and the mining town of Monticello and in the direction of the Pankey place near Nogal. To the west, the road led from Magdalena to Datil, on across Arizona to Seligman and Kingman, and finally to Yucca, near the California state line. In any direction he looked, he saw cow country—the land where he left his tracks, Ed Blanchard country.

New Mexico was Indian country for centuries before tales of treasure attracted Europeans to the area and long before the land became cow country. In the 1500s, gold, silver, and turquoise drew Spanish explorers northward from New Spain to search today's American Southwest for the fabled Seven Cities of Cíbola. Alvar Núñez Cabeza de Vaca and his three companions, one of whom was the Moorish slave Estebanico, were remnants of the ill-fated Narváez Expedition of 1528 and wandered across the wilderness for seven years. In 1536, Spanish soldiers found them near the Sinaloa River in northern Mexico and took them to the military outpost of Culiacán. From there they traveled to the city of Mexico, where Cabeza de Vaca made his report to Viceroy Antonio de Mendoza, representative of Emperor Charles V. He told the viceroy of the country and the people he had seen during the hardships of his long journey. His eyes must have sparkled when he reported signs of gold and silver in the mountains beyond New Spain and when he repeated the Indians' stories of seven large, rich cities that lay to the north. The fabled Seven Cities of Cíbola were said to be up the Río del Norte, the big river that cut through the land. He even told of trading for arrowheads made of emeralds— or of green stone, at least. He had no proof but his word; he had lost the arrowheads during a disagreement in Culiacán. No doubt Mendoza quickly made plans to send an expedition north to search for treasure. Indeed, why should he doubt the existence of riches to the north? The conquered land had proven to be very rich.

Whether hallucination or a tall tale, the story of the Seven Cities was enough to send brave men to the wilderness in search of the illusion. They did not recognize that the land's real treasure was the water of Río del Norte, the Rio Grande, which rises in the distant mountains and cuts the land from north to south before bending southeastward and flowing toward the Gulf of Mexico.

Native people of the Southwest had used the river as a highway for more than ten thousand years before the Spaniards came. It was known to Clovis Man, to people of the Folsom culture and the Mogollon culture, and to the Anasazi—the "ancient ones" who had abandoned their cliff dwellings and stone cities by the fourteenth century. Perhaps their time came to an end because of invading no-madic tribes, or maybe their departure was due to earth-parching drought, little different from the long dry spells that still plague the American Southwest.

As a result of Cabeza de Vaca's report and under orders from Vice-roy Mendoza, in 1540 Francisco Vázquez de Coronado led a party of foot soldiers, clergy, servants, and 225 horsemen northward from Compostela, near Mexico's Pacific coast, in search of Cíbola. On their return trip, the Spaniards rode along the Río del Norte's life-giving waters. Piro people, said to be descendants of the Anasazi, inhabited the fertile river valley. To the north and south of the site of the future town of Socorro were forty-five settlements and twenty-two pueblos.

Possibly twelve thousand people inhabited these villages. The Spaniards learned that the land was far from empty, but they found no Cíbola and no treasure, and there was no peace. Fierce Apaches from the southwest often swept through the settlements in lightning raids that brought death and destruction.

The first Spaniards in today's Magdalena area were a small group of soldiers and a priest who left the main body of explorers at the Rio Grande in the area where Socorro now stands. They traveled west to explore the high valley that led away from the river. They had ridden about thirty miles when they discovered a mountain with an outcropping that appeared to be the image of Mary Magdalene. The priest named the mountain La Sierra de Magdalena. The men did not linger long, however, because of harsh weather and Indians. They left and quickly rejoined the main party on the river. The land remained undisturbed for three hundred years. When Coronado returned to Mexico City in 1542, three Franciscan friars remained behind with the Indians to save souls for the Catholic Church. They were never heard of again. This land was a treacherous place.

After the explorers returned without treasure, the Spaniards decided that the northern lands were of little value. For the next forty years, the crown forgot the wild, far-flung country and left it to the grizzly bears, the mountain lions, and the dark-skinned, hostile people who inhabited it.

The Catholic Church did not forget, however. In 1580, a Franciscan missionary expedition headed by a lay brother, Fray Agustín Rodríguez, with a few soldiers under the command of Sergeant Francisco Sánchez (or Chamuscado), traveled up the Río del Norte as far north as the pueblo of Taos. Their route along the river became a portion of El Camino Real, the road to Mexico City for the next three hundred years. In 1581, the party returned to Mexico with accurate written reports of the land and its people. Even though they, too, failed to find treasure, the commander's journals rekindled Spain's interest in the area. After that, the territory was known as Nuevo Mejico— New Mexico—and Spain began its colonization of the land.

Franciscan brothers and soldiers commanded by Don Juan de Oñate led colonists up the Rio Grande in 1598. The newcomers built the first Spanish settlements and missions near the rivers and

springs. Espinosa was the first capital, but Santa Fe became the pro-
vincial capital in 1609. The Spanish government established forts
and towns, and the Franciscan brothers built churches. One of their
early missions was San Miguel, established in 1598 near the Piro
pueblo of Pilabo. It stood in the fertile Rio Grande valley east of La
Sierra de Magdalena. The church later became the center of the
Spanish town of Socorro. The mission was established in an area of
thriving pueblos watered by mountain springs. It was here that the
padres planted the first grapevines in New Mexico, and the area later
became known for its wine and its irrigated fields of wheat. San Miguel
was the central church that oversaw other missions and schools along
the river.

The presence of Spanish soldiers in the area angered the Apaches,
who stepped up their raids on the pueblos. The Franciscans abandoned the mission and then rebuilt it in 1628. The Apaches were not
the only threat to the local Indians, however. The Spaniards established their churches and forts in areas where the Indian population
was the most dense. They needed workers for their fields and for
constructing buildings. The Spanish dons and their soldiers were
above that sort of work, so the Indians were "recruited." The Pueblo
people upriver grew tired of the Spaniards' mistreatment and inter-
ference in their old ways and religion. The bloody Pueblo Revolt of
1680 drove all the Spaniards and their Indian converts down the Rio
Grande to seek asylum to the south in El Paso del Norte.

It was 1692 before the Spanish began their reconquest of New
Mexico. Don Diego de Vargas, an envoy of King Charles II, marched to
Santa Fe with a small group of soldiers and reestablished Spain's rule.
The next year, he led eight hundred settlers, soldiers, and Franciscans
from El Paso to Santa Fe. Spaniards once more occupied the capital
and rebuilt the missions. They received little help from Mexico City; a
supply train from Mexico City arrived only once every five years. Times
were hard. For 135 years, the land downriver from the town of Belen
south of Albuquerque remained abandoned, and the Apaches con-
trolled the area.

In 1816, the Spanish crown issued the Socorro Grant. Twenty-one
families colonized a block of land on the west bank of the Rio Grande.
The land grant included the site of the ruins of San Miguel Mission.

The colonists soon rebuilt the mission, and they built their adobe houses around a central plaza. Few people ventured far from town because of the ever-present Apaches as well as Navajo raiders. The Spanish colonists never traveled the high valley to the west that lay in the shadow of La Sierra de Magdalena. That land was not as benevolent as its name might indicate.

Mexico declared its independence from Spain in 1821, and life quickly changed. Where Spain had refused to open its northern borders to outsiders, Mexico welcomed the traders who made the arduous journey over the new trail to Santa Fe with much-needed goods from the distant United States. William Becknell arrived in Santa Fe with the first pack train in 1821, and Taos and Santa Fe became rowdy trade centers where all manner of men gathered. The grizzled, buckskin-clad trappers, who soon traveled the Rio Grande as they journeyed to the headwaters of the Gila in search of beavers, were equal to the Apaches who waited in ambush for them.

A trail followed the west side of the Rio Grande below Albuquerque. It went by way of the Chavez Ranch and on south past the Landrones (meaning "thieves") Mountains. The Apaches and Navajos stole horses from the settlers in the area and had hideouts in these mountains, as did later Anglo horse thieves. It paid to be wary along the river.

There were no bridges across the Rio Grande, but a crossing at Socorro gave travelers access to El Camino Real—the King's Highway—that followed the river's east bank. This route was the main trail from Santa Fe through Chihuahua and south to Mexico City. Socorro was the last settlement on the river for travelers heading south or west, and the townspeople did a brisk business in horses.

The Santa Fe Trail also brought commerce and communication to New Mexico. The trail ran to the east of Taos, so in 1835 the Mexican government granted thirty-five settlers the right to establish the town of Nuestra Señora de los Dolores de Las Vegas where the trail crossed the Gallinas River. The government instructed the settlers to build their town around a large plaza that would accommodate the steady flow of wagon trains that plied the Santa Fe Trail. Traders along the trail brought goods and wealth to many.

In 1846, the trail brought the United States Army. The well-worn ruts gave access to Mexico during the Mexican War. While in Las

Vegas in 1846, Gen. Stephen Watts Kearny declared New Mexico a territory of the United States. The town served as temporary head-quarters for the army until completion of nearby Fort Union in 1851. Then it was a supply center for the fort.

Las Vegas became a major trade center in New Mexico. By 1852, many of the merchants from Taos had moved to the more prosper-ous location. One such merchant was a French-Canadian, Michele DesMarais. In 1864 DesMarais sent to Canada for his nephew, Charles Blanchard, to join him. Then Charles, who became known as Carlos, had his younger brother, Hermas, come to New Mexico Territory to work for him. Hermas later married and had nine children, one of which was Ed Blanchard.

After the army built Fort Union, it established a whole line of forts in the Apache-controlled territory and made its presence known there. The forts remained active during the Civil War and the Apache wars that followed. Trade from Fort Craig, built in 1854 downriver from Socorro, immediately established that town as a market center.

The military presence opened the land for exploration and settle-ment. The soldiers became the first prospectors of this period. A sol-dier from Fort Craig, Pete Kinsinger, discovered silver near Pueblo Springs beneath the stony gaze of Mary Magdalene, and he staked his claim in 1863. Three years later, Col. J. S. Hutchason found lead in the Magdalena Mountains. Mines were soon in operation on the mountainside. They first produced lead and zinc. A post office and several businesses grew up between the camps and became known as Kelly. Another post office was established at Pueblo Springs and named Magdalena Mines.

Hutchason sold half his mining interest to T. B. Catron and the other half to E. W. Eaton. Eaton built a small smelter near Kelly to process ore from his mine. The other mines had to ship their ore to Socorro, and the only means of transport was by wagon, which lim-ited shipments.

Railroads linked the United States to New Mexico Territory when workers laid track for the Santa Fe line through Raton Pass to Las Vegas, Albuquerque, Socorro, San Marcial, and on toward El Paso. The rail-road reached Socorro in 1880. As early as 1878, its owners planned to run a line from Socorro west to Fort Yuma on the Colorado River.

They sent W. R. Morley to survey a route via Pueblo Springs and across the Plain of San Agustin to Fort Yuma. Morley surveyed the line as far as the west side of the plains, where rough country ended the dream. In his report to the company he recommended that the route be abandoned, but he remarked that "a portion of the country is adapted to stock raising," which later proved to be correct. No one thought of the railroad again for five years.

Mining in the Magdalena district got a boost when German-born Gustave Albert Billing arrived from Leadville, Colorado, where he had been very successful in the mining business. Billing persuaded the Atchison, Topeka & Santa Fe Railway to build a track from Socorro to the Magdalena Mining District. Next he purchased the Graphic Mine for thirty thousand dollars. Then he bought land and water rights in Park City, west of Socorro, where he built a large smelter. Billing had the first of his three furnaces in operation in September, 1883, and he was in full production in December. Silver soon replaced lead and zinc as the most important ore produced.

The New Mexico Town Company, a subsidiary of the AT&SF, laid out a town site at the railhead, and on May 8, 1884, Magdalena officially became a town. It was twenty miles west of Socorro and two thousand feet higher. It began as a supply place and wagon train terminal for ore from the mines in the nearby Kelly area. The railroad reached Magdalena in January, 1885, and a spur line ran from Magdalena to within a mile of the Kelly mine. The mines first produced lead and zinc, but Kelly's population grew to three thousand people during the 1880s, when silver was the mines' major product.

By May, 1885, workers were constructing a depot in Magdalena and had built stock pens near the tracks. Thanks to Billing, the boom was on, not only for Magdalena but also for Socorro. From Socorro's humble beginnings, who would have guessed that during the 1880s it would be the biggest, wildest, busiest town in New Mexico? It was just the place for Carlos Blanchard to extend his Las Vegas business. When he opened his meat market and mercantile store on the plaza, the store's manager was his brother, Hermas. The Socorro-Magdalena area also attracted the Kellys and the Tinguelys from Colorado. They settled in Water Canyon between Socorro and Magdalena.

*Cowboys having dinner at Water Canyon Station during a roundup on the Flat.
The AT&SF railway laid a track from Socorro to Magdalena in 1885, and
Magdalena became a major railhead for shipping the area's cattle. The train stopped
at Water Canyon Station between Socorro and Magdalena to take on water and pick
up passengers.* Courtesy J. E. Smith Collection, Socorro, New Mexico

James Patrick Kelly was no miner—he was a cowman. He was one
of many men who looked at the rich grama grass on the plains and
the lush summer pastures in the mountains and put down their roots
to stay. When the railroads arrived, the cattlemen arrived. The early
Spaniards and Mexicans had brought sheep and goats to the country, but as the mines played out, the cattlemen moved in. As in Texas,
foreign and absentee owners established large ranches. They spread
across the Plain of San Agustin south into the Black Range and the
Gila Wilderness. Ranchers trailed their cattle from these ranches and
from others in eastern Arizona to the stock pens at Magdalena, where
they loaded the animals onto trains and shipped them to Kansas City.

Some of the best cowboys in the business rode for various brands
in the area during the 1890s. Irish-born William French, who owned
the WS Ranch near the town of Alma, wrote in his book *Some Recollections of a Western Ranchman* of his foreman and cowhands who were

the best in the country. When they took his cattle to Magdalena to ship, there was no carousing in the saloons and brothels. They were well behaved. They took care of business and returned to the ranch. No doubt about it, they were professionals. However, their comings and goings from the ranch puzzled French. A man would leave for a while and a new man would take his place. Later, the first cowboy would be back on the job. As it turned out, they were Butch Cassidy and members of the Wild Bunch. They used the ranch as a hideout after they robbed a train or bank or did other mischief.

Catron County to the west of Socorro County became known as outlaw country and for good reason. Ed Blanchard grew up in the area, and he often cowboyed with men such as these. Perhaps that is why he was closemouthed about his business and that of others.

Ed Blanchard always identified with cowboys because he was one. Even though he periodically owned land, at heart he was a cowboy and not a rancher. Spur making became his obsession. It was his life as a cowboy that led to his eventual renown as a craftsman in shaping hot steel into spurs that fit a rider's boot heels.

Ed was an ordinary man, typical of his time and place, one face in many among the big-hatted, booted crowd of cowboys who rode for the large cow outfits of western New Mexico. He was generally a loner except for his strong ties to his immediate kin and to his extended family. He was especially close to the Kellys and the Cooks, because Ed's life, like theirs, was guided by the rhythm of his cow pony's gait. Ed identified with them throughout his lifetime. His life was the sum total of the times and the men who had come before him, and his personality was molded by the land. When Ed Blanchard left Water Canyon for Yucca, Arizona, and a new life in a world of business entirely foreign to him, it was as big a step for him as man's first footstep on the moon. It proved that any man can dream a dream and it will come true if he believes in himself and his ability.

Blanchard was of average height and whipcord stout. He feared no horse or cow, and that led to some terrible wrecks. Some might say those wrecks were the result of a lack of judgment and common sense. He was a solemn, quiet-spoken man with a simplicity in his expectations of life. But when he got an idea in his mind, he hung on to it with the tenacity of a grizzly bear. That was the case with spur making.

The saying goes that an acorn does not fall far from the tree. In Ed's case, the cowboy didn't fall far from the bronc. Even after he had hung up his saddle for good and began making spurs full time in his shop in Yucca, Arizona, his legs were still bowed to fit a horse's sides. Thick, black coffee still tasted better mixed with the smell of pines in the early morning air of Mount Baldy. Those days were always in his mind. The cowboy's way was Ed Blanchard's way. He might not saddle up every morning or crawl into his bedroll at night, but just ask him who he made spurs for—he made them for cowboys.

"As a young man, pulling bridle reins was my business," Blanchard told me in 1971 when I interviewed him at his shop for my book, *Cowboy Spurs and Their Makers*. But Ed Blanchard was a man of few words, and he was not well at the time. I later learned much more about him as a cowboy and a spur maker from his cousin, New Mexico rancher Tom Kelly of Water Canyon, who grew up with Ed and his friends and kinfolk. The Blanchard family's close relatives, the Kellys, taught Ed the cow business, and their neighboring rancher, Hugh Pankey, taught him to hammer hot steel into the shape of spurs that fit a cowboy's boots. Ed Blanchard took it from there.

No one can tell Ed's story better than Blanchard's cousin Tom Kelly. I have researched the times and added historical background, but the following account is based on Tom Kelly's first-hand knowledge of the country and his recollections of Ed Blanchard—cowboy and spur maker.

Part

II

As Tom Kelly Remembers

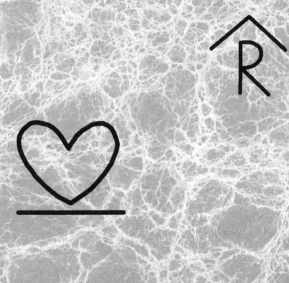

CHAPTER 2

The Road to Water Canyon

J ust as Ed Blanchard was a product of the Southwest when New Mexico was still a frontier, the spurs that he made also reflected his life and times. Blanchard's lifetime stretched from horseback days—when his livelihood was cinching his saddle on broncs and swinging his loop at wild cows—to the days when a pickup truck replaced his horse and television widened his perspective.

But to understand Ed Blanchard, it is important to learn about the Water Canyon area of New Mexico where he grew up and to know his friends and family and neighbors—good and bad. The people in this book were born in a time different from ours. Many of them were on their own most of their lives. They had to dig and scratch just to have enough to live. Even if a man did not have a family to support, life was difficult. If he had a family, times were tougher. Many people like Ed helped those who were having hard times, and they never got paid a dime for all the work they did. They didn't expect to.

Most of the old-time cowboys had a great sense of humor. They could tell you many good stories. A lot of serious things they did were remembered as big jokes that they laughed about for years. Ed was a little unusual in that he had very little humor. He seldom laughed or even grinned. He was serious in everything he did. Most of the time he was thinking about where the next dime was coming from.

People of Ed's generation were extremely loyal to their families. His father, Hermas Blanchard, died in 1908 when Ed was fourteen and left Ed's mother, Lilly Tinguely Blanchard, with nine children to rear. For years the biggest worry Ed and his brothers had was being able to send money to their mother and the children who still lived with her. Families took care of each other in those days.

People of that time were also loyal to their friends even though they sometimes had arguments. If a friend had trouble, a man took a packhorse and often rode forty or fifty miles to help. He might stay for a month to six months and work cattle. He might help a widow sell her herd so she had money and did not lose her home. Friends never expected payment for such favors.

These cowboys were gone from home with a saddle horse or two and a packhorse probably a third of their lives. They just lived out in the open in a camp someplace. They never had much money. I doubt that Ed got any wages when he was around Water Canyon working with the Kellys, but he had a place to stay and food to eat. Most ranchers could not pay wages all the time, so the cowboys often worked for food and a place to put their beds. When the ranchers did make money, they paid their help.

A lot of this country was full of wild cattle that probably belonged to local ranchers, but these cowmen didn't make much effort to catch and brand them. The cattle had grown up in these mountains and canyons, and they were wild as deer. Chasing wild cattle was how Ed and some of the other boys made their money. When a man could catch a maverick, he put his brand on it and built up a little herd of his own. That was how they became such good cowboys. Their idea was that these animals belonged to no one. If they could catch them, they were theirs. It took about twenty-five years, but in time, they cleaned the cattle out of the mountains.

After Ed's father died, Ed ran his mother's little cow herd up in the rock slides on Mount Baldy, and they were wild. It took several years to get all of the Blanchard cattle out of the mountains in order to sell a few at a time so Lilly had some money. Ed was wild on a horse; he had to be wild to catch those cattle. But that was the way he had learned to do it.

Most of these guys were kind-hearted in their own way. They would do anything for a friend. Ed never owned much, but he always had a pretty good cowboy outfit. I know at one time Ed had a saddle made by Tommy Butterfield of Butterfield Saddlery in Magdalena. It had a Rafter R $\widehat{R}$ brand on it—Ed's brand for a time. He always had two or three horses. These horses might have been given to him. A horse might be so damn mean no one wanted it, or it might be a stray horse and no one knew who it belonged to. If the owner came by and recognized his horse, the cowboy gave it back, but sometimes he rode it for years.

Back during that time, there were no fences. If a cowboy bought or traded for a horse and took it to a new country, sometimes that horse tried to go home. He might get to a ranch and stop, and they'd use him until the owner came along and claimed him. That's how Ed got a lot of horses that he rode.

Most traveling in those days was by horseback. Many cowboys we knew would come by and spend two or three days. They had a packhorse with a bed, a few groceries, and a couple of small Dutch ovens. They always had a pistol and an old .30-30 rifle for protection. They just drifted around for a month or more when they weren't working. Ed did that.

Many of the people Ed knew when he was young were old outlaws. A lot of them came from Texas and settled in this country. Some were from Indian Territory—Oklahoma. They came west because they had been in trouble, but they stayed in New Mexico and established ranches, and most of them were pretty good people. A lot were known by one name, and after they were here several years and it was safe, they began using their real names. Of course, no one talked about this. You didn't ask them why or where they came from. If you were smart, you didn't ask any questions. That's how it was during Ed Blanchard's time in Water Canyon.

Being a cowboy who never strayed far from his bedground, Ed Blanchard was more of a product of his environment than of his

Charles George Tinguely, Ed Blanchard's grandfather,
in 1881 when the Tinguelys lived near Gunnison, Colorado.
Courtesy Tom Kelly

international background. Ed's maternal grandfather, Charles George Tinguely, was born in 1822 in Bern, Switzerland. He was of French descent and spoke French, German, and English. During his years in New Mexico, he learned to speak Spanish by being around the people of Mexican descent. His trade was that of a dairyman. He made and sold cheese and all kinds of dairy products, but he was also a wine maker.

Ed's German grandmother, Anna Barbara Schwab, was also born in Bern. She was ten years younger than George Tinguely. They came to the United States on the same ship in 1854 and married shortly after. She spoke German, French, some Spanish, and broken English.

George and Anna acquired a herd of milk cows and settled on a 320-acre farm near Lincoln, Nebraska. Their first two children were born there. The first, Louis, was born in 1857 and evidently died as an infant, for none of the other Tinguely children knew of him. Next was my grandmother, Mary Ann, born in 1859. The Tinguelys eventually had four children who lived to be adults.

George Tinguely apparently had itchy feet, and he had a plan. He leased the family farm in Nebraska in 1860, and with his wife and daughter and his milk cows and a herd of horses, he followed the railroad as it was built westward. There were large camps of laborers at the railheads, so Tinguely stopped near the camps, milked his cows, and sold milk, butter, and cheese. He also stopped near the army forts. He found good markets for his products. He must have had several wagons and men to help with the horses and cattle.

They reached Colorado and stopped for a while near the new town of Denver. George filed on 320 acres, but they didn't stay long. They moved on to South Pueblo, a town that is no more. Charles Albert was born there on the Tinguely Ranch in 1864. Two years later, Lilly was born. Her place of birth is uncertain—perhaps there or maybe in New Mexico.

According to a family story, while in South Pueblo Tinguely became acquainted with a Texas cattleman—either Charles Goodnight or John Chisum. Both men were in and out of Colorado and had established ranches on the Pecos River in New Mexico Territory. They sold cattle to the army to feed the Navajos and Apaches on the Bosque Redondo Reservation. The Indians lived under the watchful eyes of the soldiers from nearby Fort Sumner and Fort Stanton on the Rio Bonito. Few cattle and supplies reached the Indians because of the agent's shady dealings, and the Mescaleros left the reservation in 1866. Many of the Navajos starved.

Charles Goodnight and Oliver Loving found a ready market in New Mexico and Colorado for the Texas cattle they drove up the treacherous Goodnight Trail. They established the Bosque Grande Ranch on the Pecos River, forty miles below Fort Sumner, as a holding ground for their cattle until they sold them. Loving was killed by Comanches in 1867, but Goodnight still used the Bosque Grande range as a rest stop for his herds going north.

[21]

The Bosque Redondo Reservation was closed in 1868, when the government signed a new treaty with the Navajos and returned the remnants of the tribe to their homeland in northwestern New Mexico and northeast Arizona. The army abandoned Fort Sumner and sold the land and buildings at auction in 1870.

John Chisum sometimes sold cattle to Charles Goodnight and later was a part owner of some of the herds Goodnight sold and delivered to Colorado buyers. One of Goodnight's major buyers in Colorado was John W. Iliff, who became one of the West's leading cattlemen. In fact, in 1868 Goodnight delivered to Iliff the first herd of Texas cattle to arrive in Wyoming. Either Chisum or Goodnight told George Tinguely of the fertile valley along the Hondo River in New Mexico Territory and of Las Placitas del Rio Bonito, the village known as Lincoln after the county of the same name was established in 1869.

Tinguely moved his family there with the idea of furnishing milk and cheese to the army at nearby Fort Stanton and to the settlers who were expected in the new county. However, the closing of the reservation in 1868 and of Fort Sumner gave free rein to the disgruntled Apaches who had left the reservation earlier. Raiding parties led by Geronimo and Victorio laid waste to the countryside, and the settlers who were already there packed up and left. George Tinguely's business dwindled, and after Sam was born in 1869, the family returned to Colorado. This time they stopped for a while near Trinidad.

Another man who went to the Lincoln, New Mexico, area to make his fortune as a trader was a twenty-two-year-old French-Canadian named Charles Blanchard. When the Apaches became troublesome, Blanchard remarked that he did not wish to "leave my bones there," so he returned north to Las Vegas, a major trade center where his uncle, Michele DesMarais, was in the mercantile business. It is probable that Blanchard and Tinguely were acquainted in Lincoln County. They certainly were at a later date.

The Tinguelys remained near Trinidad, Colorado, until 1875, when they joined six or seven other families who traveled west to the Gunnison River country. There, Sylvester Richardson organized a town company and founded the town of Gunnison on the eastern edge of the twelve-million-acre Ute Reservation. Soon after, prospectors found gold and silver in the area. The U.S. Senate had granted the land to the Indians "forever"—or at least until someone discovered gold and silver. Of the group who arrived from Trinidad, only two families stayed. One of them was the Tinguelys.

George Tinguely settled above town on a large tract of land where Ohio Creek empties into the Gunnison River. He had a big farm, and of course, he had milk cows and made cheese, but he also raised horses. There was a good market for his products, especially after 1879, when Gunnison began its mining boom and settlers poured into the country. By 1880, Gunnison was a prosperous town.

When the Tinguelys first arrived in the Gunnison area, my grandpa, James Patrick Kelly of Virginia, was already there and had been there for some time. He had an Indian trading post, and he and several other men cared for the government livestock on the Ute Reservation. He was there when settlers first began arriving in 1869. He and a partner had homesteaded a good-sized chunk of land, and it is said that they donated 120 acres for the town of Gunnison. They also had a post office and a large herd of their own cattle. J. P. Kelly was pretty well off when Charles Tinguely came to that country.

Grandpa Kelly spied Mary Ann when the Tinguelys first arrived in 1875. She was sixteen years old, and he decided he was going to marry her. He had been there seven or eight years, and he probably hadn't seen a white woman for some time. According to the stories told, the couple wanted to be married, and the old man balked and had a fit. One story is that Grandpa Kelly drove up to the house in his little home-made sleigh and pulled a gun on George Tinguely. Grandpa took Mary Ann to the shack of a miner who was a justice of the peace, and they were married in 1878.

Probably the true story was that J. P. hung around the Tinguelys' place until the old man got his whistle wet on wine, because Grandpa Tinguely was a pretty good wine drinker. Then the couple ran off and were married. Anyway, the marriage lasted, and they had several kids.

Fate took a further hand in George Tinguely's life in 1880. The country had a five- or six-foot snowfall that winter. George's cattle were in the fields and along the river bottom. They became snowbound, and he couldn't get to them with hay. Most of them died of starvation. Then in 1881, the Denver and Rio Grande Railroad arrived in

J. P. Kelly, Tom Kelly's grandfather, at the Kelly Ranch on the Flat in about 1932. Courtesy Tom Kelly

Gunnison, and the government removed the Utes from land they had been granted "forever." The Indian lands would be open for filing in June of 1882. However, the Utes had barely left before homesteaders began staking claims.

J. P. Kelly was out of a job. The Kellys' two children had died during the harsh winter, and Kelly, like Tinguely, was ready to leave the cold country. Both men sold their land. The story is that Grandpa

[24]

Tinguely sold his place for ninety thousand dollars. The two families traveled south into New Mexico in 1881. Grandpa Tinguely always looked for a place of opportunity. This time it was the Socorro area, down the Rio Grande from Albuquerque. But his choice of location was more than happenstance. When the railroad arrived in Socorro, it became a boom town and a leading trade center.

The Santa Fe Railway had reached Las Vegas in 1879, and it changed the way the merchants did business. The train whistle was the death knell of the freighting and transportation business on the Santa Fe Trail. Goods, passengers, and mail were now brought from the East by rail. The railroad soon reached Albuquerque, where it turned west to California. A branch was laid south through Socorro and on toward El Paso. The Socorro area looked like the promised land to Tinguely and Kelly, as it did to Charles Blanchard.

In April, 1880, gold was found near the town of White Oaks, eighty miles or so east of Socorro. Another mining town, Kelly, was west of Socorro in the Magdalena Mountains. In 1863, a soldier had discovered traces of silver near Pueblo Springs and staked his claim. Prospectors swarmed in, and miners developed their diggings. Their nearby camp became the town of Kelly. The mines produced silver, lead, zinc, and copper until they were finally closed in the 1940s. During peak production, Kelly had a population of three thousand inhabitants. The Santa Fe Railway laid a track from Socorro west to the Magdalena Mining District to haul ore from the mines to the new smelter in Socorro. The town of Magdalena grew up at the railhead. Socorro was the bustling supply center for these mining operations.

When J. P. Kelly arrived in the area in 1880 or 1881, he stopped only briefly in Socorro. He was no merchant or miner; he was a cowman. He moved on west to Water Canyon in the Magdalena Mountains. The high flat land east of the future site of Magdalena and the grasslands of the Plain of San Agustin to its southwest were more to his liking. They were good grazing lands for cattle.

Tinguely remained in the Socorro area and first settled north of the town near Polvadera. He had brought what was left of his milk cow herd as well as two hundred mares and some stallions. He bought two or three pieces of land that he planned to irrigate and farm. The

Indians practiced irrigation long before the white settlers came to the area. The Spaniards brought a similar technique to North America that they had learned from the Moors. It was a simple system of *acequias* or ditches that carried water from the river. But the railroad cut off Tinguely's supply of irrigation water from the Rio Grande. His farmland was no good without water. He sued the railroad, and, of course, he lost.

Tinguely also built a home in Water Canyon, which was twenty-five miles from Polvadera. Evidently the family spent time in each place. After Tinguely's irrigation problems at the Polvadera place, Grandpa moved his mares to Revechi. They hadn't been there but a few months when the horses ate locoweed, and many of them died. After that, the Tinguelys moved to Water Canyon and stayed. However, according to Socorro County records of 1886, Grandma Tinguely bought thirty-four acres of irrigated land with six thousand grapevines near Socorro. The area was noted for its wine, and of course, Grandpa Tinguely was a wine maker. Anna Tinguely bought this land from Hermas Blanchard, who had become her son-in-law. So the Tinguelys continued to have interests in the Socorro-Polvadera area even though they lived in Water Canyon.

The Kelly Ranch headquartered in Water Canyon and was in full swing in 1882. James P. Kelly was a pioneer rancher in Socorro County, and he eventually established J. P. Kelly & Sons, a ranching partnership with his boys. He branded a double half circle ◠◠ on the left ribs of his cattle. Grandpa Kelly registered that brand in Monticello on March 3, 1883. The brand was passed to my father, Frank Kelly, and his brother, Jim, and they gave it to me in the 1950s.

James P. Kelly's horse brand was the JK Connected ⅄ on the left hip. Grandma Kelly's cattle brand was T on the left shoulder, a Bar on the ribs, and Lazy T ⊤—⊣ on the hip. The Kellys also used EUX on the left shoulder, ribs, and hip—and the W Pitchfork, which ran from the shoulder to the hip on the left side. The old-timers said that these big brands all over a cow's side were hard for a cow thief to rework. They were also easy to see from a distance and in a herd.

Grandpa Kelly built his house up Water Canyon a mile and a half above the settlement to get away from everyone else. The house and the kitchen behind it were both two-storied and made of big logs. It was just up the hill overlooking the creek. Grandpa Kelly and Grandpa Tinguely, with the help of local men, Dad McDonald and Charlie Gay, built a little pie-shaped rock furnace and made lime. They used lime to make paint and also to chink the logs. The house had a living room and a bedroom downstairs. The kids slept upstairs over the kitchen, and their parents slept downstairs in the main house. To reach the second floor, the family went up outside steps at the side of the house.

The canyon was belly-deep in grass and full of large trees. It was open country, too, since the numerous deer kept the scrub eaten down. The creek always ran with water, fed by springs in the mountains. As people moved into the canyon, they diverted water to the various houses by way of ditches.

The Kellys ran their cattle in the mountains and on the plains outside of the canyon. That area was known as the Flat. It was open range and had no fences. It was good cattle country. The native grasses on the Flat still include Texas timothy and blue and black grama, but only the blue grama grows in the mountains. Water was the most valuable asset in the area. A rancher could buy forty acres with a spring of water on it, but the squatters would come in with cattle, and soon that spring would be watering a thousand head. The animals quickly ate all the grass, and the local cowman was grazed out.

Worse than the cattle were the sheepmen who wandered around the country with thousands of sheep in their large flocks. The government established the Forest Service in 1905, and in 1908, the local cattlemen asked the Forest Service to manage the land in this area. Then the Bureau of Land Management—the BLM—took over management of all government land outside the forest boundary. The people in Water Canyon had permits to live and graze animals there, and most of them had mining claims in the area, too. The Forest Service did not pay much attention to who was running on the land, so long as they didn't have sheep. They figured sheep ruined the country. The BLM's handling of the situation worked fine in the beginning.

The Flat was a different situation; there was no private land there. The Santa Fe Railway had built a track from Socorro to Magdalena in

1884. Some of the Flat belonged to the railroad and the rest was government land. Grandpa Kelly at first leased the land he used on the Flat. Then my father, Frank Kelly, homesteaded the land adjoining an old lakebed on the Flat in 1913. The lake only had water in it every twelve or fifteen years, so Pop drilled a well, and soon he watered all the cattle in the country. Pop took an old log cabin to the Flat from up in the canyon and proved up his land. When Uncle Jim was old enough, Pop filed on a section for him, too. All the Kelly cattle ran together at that time. Grandpa Kelly and his sons kept the ranch intact until his death in 1934, when the estate was divided among his children.

The Blanchards also became intertwined with the Tinguelys and the Kellys. But a Blanchard was in New Mexico Territory long before the 1880s, when George Tinguely first made wine and cheese near Socorro and J. P. Kelly's cattle bedded down in the meadows on Mount Baldy and grazed the Flat outside the mouth of Water Canyon. In fact, the first of the Blanchard kin to arrive, the French-Canadian Michele DesMarais, had left his home in Quebec and come to the Mexican trading center of Taos in 1837.

Many French-Canadians left their homeland that year because of the Patriots War, and they traveled to the American West via the Santa Fe Trail. The trail was the lifeline from the United States east of the Mississippi River to the trade center of Santa Fe. After 1849, a stage-coach line followed the route. However, the harsh weather and rampaging Indians made it a hazardous journey. After the United States acquired California and other northern provinces of Mexico following the Mexican War, Congress made New Mexico a U.S. territory in 1850. Fort Union, twenty-seven miles north of the village of Las Vegas, was established in 1851 as protection for settlers of the area and travelers on the Santa Fe Trail. The fort became headquarters for the Military Department of New Mexico and served as the supply base for fifty or so smaller forts throughout the Southwest.

The importance of Taos as a trade center diminished as Las Vegas increased its own trade and stature. By 1852, many of the Taos merchants, including DesMarais, had moved southeast to the village of Las Vegas. The town quickly became an important freighting and mercantile center for the Southwest, and Michele DesMarais—or Miguel, as he was now known—became a prosperous merchant.

In 1864, DesMarais sent for his nephew, twenty-two-year-old Charles Blanchard of St. Marc, Quebec. The young man's parents, Margaret and Charles Blanchard, Sr., must have thought this a grand opportunity for their son to learn the mercantile business. The elder Blanchard was a farmer, and he had been a soldier in the Patriots War.

Young Charles went to Saint Louis, where another uncle, Elzear Blanchard, was also a successful merchant. Then he traveled to New Mexico Territory via the Santa Fe Trail. Charles worked for a brief time as a clerk in DesMarais's store in Las Vegas before he left in 1864 to establish his own trading business in Rio Bonito, now called Lincoln. Las Vegas, 110 miles to the north of the Bosque Redondo Reservation, was the reservation's nearest supply point, but Rio Bonito was closer to Bosque Redondo. Perhaps DesMarais thought to bypass competition in Las Vegas by having Charles establish a store in Rio Bonito. The town was destined to later become a trade center and the site of the notorious Lincoln County War, which was a merchants' war.

Blanchard, like the Tinguelys, was in the right place at the wrong time and soon found it a hotbed rather than the promised land. After three years of evading Apaches and guarding his scalp, Charles returned to Las Vegas in 1868. The closing of the Bosque Redondo Reservation and of Fort Sumner escalated the Apache raids. Blanchard and the Tinguelys left the country, as did many other settlers.

After Charles—or Carlos, as he was now called—returned to Las Vegas, he was a jack-of-all-trades for a short time, but he soon became wagon master of an ox train that plied the Santa Fe Trail. Traders still carried on a lively business in Saint Louis goods, and the freighters also kept busy hauling army supplies to and from Fort Union. Blanchard, like other traders such as the Romero brothers, kept ox trains constantly going and coming on the Santa Fe Trail.

In 1868, Blanchard had a government contract to haul supplies to Fort Union. The railroad was building across Kansas toward Denver, so Carlos drove his ox train back up the Santa Fe Trail to meet the Kansas Pacific tracks and pick up the supplies. He met a party of freighters who told him that the rails had reached Fort Harker in the

Blanchard's uncle, Carlos Blanchard of Las Vegas.
The Blanchards were French Canadians and Carlos was a
successful merchant and dealer in mining properties.
Courtesy Linda Blanchard Whitaker

Smoky Hill River valley in central Kansas near today's Ellsworth. Blanchard's ox train arrived there, loaded the government supplies, and returned to Fort Union without incident.

Carlos had enough time left that season to make a second trip to pick up goods from Saint Louis for his Las Vegas store. He loaded his ox train with loose wool to sell and returned to Fort Harker in mid-July. While he waited for his supplies to arrive, he sold his wool and traded his ox outfit and two thousand dollars for sixty-six mules and harness and ten wagons ready for the trail. A mule train could cover the miles faster than oxen, and Blanchard's train could be back in Las Vegas in twenty-five days. However, he didn't figure on Indian trouble. It had been four years since Colonel Chivington and his troops attacked a peaceful Cheyenne village in Colorado, an incident that became known as the Sand Creek Massacre. During the summer of 1868, leaders of several of the Plains tribes signed the Medicine Lodge Treaty, but the government's promises of food and supplies were slow in coming and the Indians were restless.

When Blanchard's goods arrived, his men loaded them in their wagons and started for home. Four days west of Fort Dodge, the freighters unhitched their mules and made camp for the night. Suddenly, one hundred war-painted Indians swept down out of the hills, and the four men who guarded the mule herd barely escaped with their lives. The Indians drove off all the mules and Carlos's saddle horse in a cloud of dust. Supplies were intact and no one was hurt, but the men were left afoot with their wagons at a standstill. Blanchard set out alone to walk the fifty miles back to Fort Dodge for help. He arrived one morning at sunrise. The fort's commander sent help and enough stock with him to bring the wagons and men back to the fort. However, the officer would not let the teamsters stay near the fort. He required that they camp two miles to the east.

Blanchard sent word to Las Vegas via the military telegraph. While they awaited help from New Mexico, they often endured running battles with the Indians riding through their camp. Finally, on October 12, after a small group of men from Las Vegas arrived safely with mules, horses, and oxen, Carlos and his party were ready to depart.

When Blanchard reported to the commander at the fort that he and his train were leaving, the officer informed him that they could not go. If they attempted to do so, he would hold him in jail all winter, if necessary. However, if Carlos could prove he was owner or part owner of the merchandise he was hauling and would sign a release waiving all claims against the government for any losses, they would be free to go to their doom. Blanchard convinced him the supplies were for his store. The officer said he could send no escort with the train, but he lent the men twenty rifles and some ammunition. He asked that they return the rifles to Fort Lyon in Colorado Territory if the train got through.

The freighters' return trip was hair-raising, but the men made it safely. The plaza at Las Vegas was a welcome sight.

Carlos Blanchard often went on buying trips to Saint Louis and evidently made a lot of money in freighting and the mercantile business in Las Vegas. Blanchard & Company occupied a long, one-story building on the east side of the plaza. A similar store, H. Romero & Brother, was located next door. The back door of each store opened onto vegetable gardens that ran down to the river and were irrigated by *acequias*. Carlos's uncle, Miguel DesMarais, owned a meat market and hardware store on the plaza, and Blanchard also had a warehouse nearby. Carlos married Estella Romero. He had the first telephone in New Mexico Territory installed in 1879, between the Blanchard store and his home.

However, about that time, Carlos and most of the plaza merchants in Las Vegas suffered business reverses caused by a long drought and the crumbling of the merchant credit system. Since there were no banks, a barter system had been established between landowners and merchants, who acted as moneylenders and advanced the landowners cash and credit on their future products. Therefore, the drought broke many of the merchants as well as the landowners.

Also, in 1879 the Raynolds brothers established a small bank on the plaza. It became a national bank and the forerunner of the First National Bank of Albuquerque and the First National Bank of El Paso. New banking methods from the East replaced the old system. Perhaps these changes led to Carlos Blanchard's interest in expanding his business to Socorro, where he opened a second store and put his younger brother, Hermas, in charge. No one recalls when Hermas left Canada and arrived in New Mexico, but he was in Socorro in 1879. Carlos must have considered the drought a temporary setback, for he continued his mercantile business in Las Vegas.

Las Vegas remained his home, and Carlos was active in the town's civic affairs as well as those of New Mexico Territory. Blanchard was one of several partners who built the Plaza Hotel that opened in 1882 on Old Town Plaza. The historic hostelry still welcomes guests after more than a century. Blanchard was also instrumental in establishing roads in 1880 and providing water for the new gold-mining town of White Oaks, 180 miles to the south. He foresaw a glorious future in the development of New Mexico's mineral resources. He was one of five men who formed the Las Vegas & St. Louis Mining & Smelting Company, incorporated on March 12, 1880. Charles Blanchard was listed as president and treasurer. The company owned mines and claims in the Silver Mountain Mining District of Water Canyon in the Magdalena Mountains, as well as others in the San Antonio, Limitar, and Polvadera districts.

By 1884, many of the mines had proved worthless or too expensive to develop, and the various shareholders began transferring their stock to Charles Blanchard. Carlos was not discouraged. He continued to speculate in mineral and oil leases until his death in 1914.

Carlos purchased a slaughterhouse and meat market in Socorro in 1887. After that, his stores went by the name Blanchard Meat and Supply Company, as did his mining investments. In the 1880s, Socorro became a major supply center for the area. Hermas dabbled in mineral leases and took care of store business while Carlos was away on buying and selling trips. The Blanchard store in Socorro was on the plaza and carried all manner of goods, including Giant Powder, which was dynamite. The barns, stable, and slaughterhouse were located at the corner of Plaza and Court Streets.

Hermas Blanchard (left) *in the Blanchard Meat Market in Socorro in the late 1880s. Man at right is thought to be Carlos Blanchard.*
Courtesy J. E. Smith Collection, Socorro, New Mexico

Hermas Blanchard (in white apron) *is seen in the center of a group of townsmen gathered on the sidewalk in front of the Blanchard Meat & Supply Co.'s store buildings on Socorro's plaza.* Courtesy J. E. Smith Collection, Socorro, New Mexico

Carlos bought and traded mining claims and land. He owned property in and around Socorro and had mining interests in both Chloride, New Mexico, and Kelly, as well as in Water Canyon. The Blanchards were good promoters. They bought claims, kept them a while, and then sold them. They built buildings on much of their land, so they helped settle Socorro County. They made good money from their dealings. By 1904, Carlos had oil and coal leases in Utah's San Juan Basin, and he worked to bring a railroad to Farmington, New Mexico, to service his holdings in that area. Although he had business interests throughout New Mexico and at times stayed in Farmington and Las Cruces, his home remained in Las Vegas.

Hermas Blanchard met Lilly Tinguely in Socorro, and she was eighteen when they married on January 27, 1884. It did not appear that George Tinguely objected to Blanchard marrying one of his younger daughters. That wasn't the case when Grandpa Kelly married my grandmother, Mary Ann Tinguely, in Colorado, however. Back in those

Ed's father, Hermas Blanchard, in 1884. Hermas and Lillian "Lilly" Tinguely Blanchard had nine children when Hermas died of pneumonia in 1908. Courtesy Linda Blanchard Whitaker

days, I guess he hated to lose his kids because they milked the cows. Five kids milking cows could squirt a lot of milk.

Hermas and Lilly owned a house in Socorro where they lived for a while. Later, after they moved to Water Canyon and had children old enough to be in high school, Lilly and the children often stayed in town in a house her father had given her. The school in Water Canyon had only lower grades. Perhaps Lilly's house in Socorro was the same one where the couple lived when they were first married.

Hermas and Lilly lived in Water Canyon and had been married for twenty-four years when Hermas died in 1908. They had had ten children—five girls and five boys—but Sam, who was born in 1902, died when he was a year or two old. Charlie was the oldest. He was born in Socorro in 1886. All the rest were born in Water Canyon. After Charlie came Josephine, Agnes, Rose, Edward, Lillian, Arthur, Sam, Katherine, and Paul. Katherine never married and Charlie remained a bachelor. Ed wasn't married until he was seventy-two years old, and that didn't take.

Edward Fred Blanchard was born at home in Water Canyon, where the family moved in the late 1880s. The Blanchards had a four- or five-room L-shaped house—a nice house for the times. They had a large yard and a big garden, and they raised a lot of fruit. The orchard had two big cherry trees, two apricot trees, four apple trees, and several peach trees. They irrigated the place by a ditch that brought water from the creek above the house. It ran through the yard and around the house.

Lilly always had chickens and pigs and milk cows. And she had a herd of sixty to one hundred head of cattle that she ran up in the mountains. The cows were hers and never Hermas's. She branded them Rafter R ℞ on the ribs.

The settlement in Water Canyon was fairly good-sized. From one hundred to two hundred people lived in the area. Cabins dotted the canyons and the hillsides. A store with the school in the back was in the main part of town. There was also a post office after 1903. Everyone raised vegetables and watered them out of the creek.

The Blanchards moved into this conglomeration of people. They all had mining claims and holes they dug in. When they ran out of

*When Hermas Blanchard died in 1908, his wife, Lilly Tinguely
Blanchard, was left with nine children to rear. Ed was fourteen and
the Kellys taught him the cowboy trade.* Courtesy Tom Kelly

money, they went over the mountain to the town of Kelly and worked
in the mines for six months or a year. Then they came back and dug
in their holes again, looking for gold or some sign of minerals. They
found a showing in every hole they dug, but no one ever hit it big.

Silver had been mined at Kelly since the 1860s. During the 1880s,
Kelly was the most prosperous mining town in central New Mexico. In
1903, it became a major source of zinc carbonate, a vital ingredient in

paint. But the main ones who benefited from the mining business were
the promoters. There might have been some rich minerals in the area,
but it was the crooks and promoters who made the most money.

One promoter was an expert at getting eastern money. He would
go back to New York and gather a bunch of people who had money
and come out here and start one of these mines. They'd spend several thousand dollars and give up. Then the promoter would go get
another bunch and start over again. That is what happened to the
mining business in Water Canyon.

Like everyone else in the area, Hermas had some mining claims
on top of a hill up Water Canyon. It is on record that he sold three
claims to Margarita Blanchard, who lived in Las Vegas, for three thousand dollars in 1895. They all dug in their mines, but they never got
much that amounted to anything.

What no one understood at the time was that New Mexico's geol-
ogy made gold mining unprofitable. Gold was formed in bedrock
layers by the solidification of magma masses, and prospectors found
fingers of rich gold but never the mother lode. They dug along the
veins only to find the gold suddenly ended, interrupted by metamor-
phic limestone or sandstone or slate. Uplifts and faulting fragmented
the veins. The expense of lode mining was so great that the return
was not profitable.

Because of the shortage of streams in the state, placer mining was
also out of the question since it requires water. Therefore, New Mexico
has never been an important gold-mining state. The town of Kelly
was established in the 1860s and by the 1870s, its mines produced
silver, zinc, and lead. A German named Billing built a smelter in
Socorro that had three blast furnaces and was a big operation for the
times. Freighters hauled ore down to Socorro by wagon until a railroad was completed in 1885 to carry ore from the Magdalena area to
Socorro. Billing built a spur from Magdalena to the mines and from
the tracks in Socorro to his smelter. Magdalena became an important railhead for shipping thousands of cattle and sheep as well as
ore. It was soon a rip-roaring frontier town.

The sixteen-mile railroad between Socorro and Magdalena was
called "the elevator." It climbed two thousand feet up canyons, through
malpais outcroppings and great reddish-colored rocks, to top out on

a high plateau—the wide, grassy La Jencia Plain east of Magdalena. That was the area the Kellys called the Flat. The railroad built a station and a barn and corrals by the tracks near the mouth of Water Canyon. The train stopped there to pick up passengers and to take on water for the engine.

The railroad men dug a well in Water Canyon and hit water twenty-five feet down. They covered the well with a round, cement-like dome. A pipeline from the dome carried water six miles down the canyon to an overhead tank at the station. Every morning, the train stopped at the station to take on water. A dirt tank below the overhead tank caught the overflow water. Grandpa Kelly had a ninety-nine-year water lease from the railroad for the overflow from the tank.

The railroad made travel to town easier. Everyone who lived in Water Canyon still had a horse or a team, and some had a wagon and a few burros. On the whole, they were a self-sufficient bunch. They all had chickens and goats, sheep and pigs. They didn't have to work too hard. They could always eat what was running around loose. There were often arguments and fights about who owned what, but all in all they seemed to get along and to get by.

CHAPTER 3

The Making of a Cowboy

Edward Fred Blanchard was born in Water Canyon on September 26, 1894. Ol' Ed was like any kid—he wasn't an angel. He ran around over the mountainsides just like the rest of them and messed in his pants and peed in his britches. My grandmother Tinguely taught school in Water Canyon in 1896 and 1897. She had Ed's older brothers and sisters in school, but she didn't have Ed. He wasn't old enough.

Ed, like my dad and his brother Jim, went to school down the canyon in the little red board schoolhouse on top of Ranger Station Hill. The teacher stayed at the ranger station and walked over the hill to the schoolhouse. There's no hill there anymore. It's been leveled off. When the community quit using the school, Uncle Jim, Ed, and Pop hauled the building in a wagon down to the Flat to use as a bunkhouse on the Kelly Ranch. That was sometime after 1918.

Forest ranger Steve Garst was sent to Water Canyon by the Forest Service about 1910. He lived at the ranger station and became a great friend of my dad's. The ranger station was a three-bedroom house with a big kitchen and a living room and a large front porch and a back porch. It was made of adobe. In 1939, the Conservation Corps tore it down and built the little rock cabin that is there now.

I never heard where Steve Garst was from, but his father was a politician in Washington, D.C. Much later, Steve and a friend in the Forest Service became partners in a herd of cattle. They ran them on land acquired with a forest permit, and Steve was fired by the department. His father managed to get him reinstated, and then he retired.

The last Blanchard child was Paul, who was born in Water Canyon in 1907 in the same house where Ed was born. Hermas dug up a white fir tree up the canyon and planted it in his yard when Paul was born. The house is now gone, but the tree's still there.

Times must have been hard about then, for Hermas worked in the mines at Kelly. Lilly and Hermas mortgaged fourteen two- and three-year-old steers to the Ranch Supply Company in Magdalena for $354. Maybe it was for a bill they couldn't pay or a draw for supplies. The Becker-Mactavish store acted as the "Territorial and Country Depository" and was later considered the first bank in town. However, the merchants often advanced people money or credit to live on until time came to sell their cattle or wool. Possibly that was what the Blanchards' note was for. That practice was not unusual.

My dad said Hermas was a hard worker and a walker. The Blanchards lived in Water Canyon while Hermas worked in the mines in Kelly. He walked to work up this long canyon to the top of the divide between here and Kelly. It is five miles to the top of the ridge and about three thousand feet higher. Kelly is two thousand feet down on the other side. Hermas walked back and forth to work. Most of the time, he stayed in Kelly during the week and came home on the weekends. He always walked; he never rode a horse.

The older Kelly boys worked in Kelly in those days, too. They lived two miles up the canyon above the Blanchards, but they always rode. They hobbled their horses out during the week, and then they'd catch them and ride back home on their days off. But Hermas walked and kept pace with them and never stopped to rest.

As I earlier stated, apparently Grandpa Charles Tinguely had no objection to Hermas Blanchard marrying Lilly. However, as time went by and the old man was in his eighties, he became grouchy. The

*Nothing is left of the Blanchard place in Water Canyon except a white fir tree
that Hermas dug up in the canyon and planted in the yard when Paul,
the youngest, was born in 1906. He was born in the room where Ed had
been born twelve years earlier. Pictured here are the Blanchard barns
and corrals that were behind the house.* Courtesy Tom Kelly

original Tinguely house in Water Canyon was about halfway between
the Kelly house and the Blanchard place on a little flat by the side of
the road. When Grandpa Tinguely got old and grouchy, Grandma
wouldn't live with him. To be near her daughter, she stayed in a small
board house just around the hill from the Kelly home, and that's
where she was living when she died in 1914. Grandpa Tinguely finally
moved up there toward the end of his life after he developed palsy.
The house is gone now, but Pop said it faced the road and had three
rooms and a porch across the front.

Originally, everyone went up the creek horseback, but when my
father bought a Model T that he called Bluebonnet, Bluebonnet
couldn't navigate the rocks and snow in the bottom of the canyon.
Grandpa Kelly built a road on the hillside along the creek and then
he paid Charlie Blanchard to build the road on up to the Kelly house.

Then Pop could drive on up there. From then on, that part of the road was called Charlie's Hill.

Hermas Blanchard went tripping up this road one day to visit the Kellys, and he stayed there quite a while. When he left that afternoon, he came chunking off back down the road and he walked by Old Man Tinguely's house. Tinguely was sitting in a chair out on his porch, leaning back against the wall. His two dogs lay on the porch beside him. Hermas went right on by and didn't say a word to him. The old man hollered something at him, but Hermas still didn't answer, so Tinguely sicced his dogs on him.

The fight started, and the dogs tore Hermas's pants off and bit him several times. Hermas finally got the dogs kicked off and went on down the creek to his house. About two hours later, he showed up again and called Tinguely's dogs down the road and shot them both. I don't guess Tinguely and Hermas got along too good after that.

In 1908, Lilly got word that Hermas had died of pneumonia in Kelly. The flu and pneumonia were prevalent in those days. Lilly and the children went to Kelly to bury Hermas, since there was no cemetery in Water Canyon. Years later when Ed was old, he came back to Water Canyon and wanted me to go with him to the Kelly Cemetery. He wanted to put a tombstone on his father's grave. Ed was only fourteen years old when Hermas died, and when we got to the cemetery, he couldn't remember where his father was buried. We never found the grave. However, the grave has since been located.

Grandpa Tinguely died a year after Grandma died. They both died in the downstairs bedroom at the Kelly place and were buried up the canyon above the house. Grandpa had dozed off in his chair and dropped his pipe, which set fire to some wood shavings beside the fireplace. He was badly burned and lived only a day or two.

While the Blanchards lived in Water Canyon, Lilly had milk cows, chickens, and pigs. She also acquired a little cow herd. Before she left in 1919, she had about fifty cows and two or three good milk cows. Lilly was having a hard time making ends meet, and her house was sold for the taxes owed—$43.53. My Grandmother Kelly bought her cows and the Rafter R brand as well as the house and barn. Lilly gathered up what kids were left at home and moved to El Paso, where some of the Blanchards lived. We still milked some of her cows when I was a little kid. They carried that Rafter R brand on the left ribs. Lilly also branded LB.

One time about 1952, my dad and I were up the canyon gathering cattle. There was a yearling up in a little cut in the bluffs above the creek. It was so steep I couldn't get to him horseback, so I climbed up there on foot and ran him down. When he started down the cut, he kicked up a monstrous cowbell. I picked it up and packed it down to the bottom of the canyon.

My dad was sitting on his horse there. "Good gosh!" he said. "You found Aunt Lilly's milk cow's bell. We hunted a whole month for that thing."

Sure enough, it had the initials LB chiseled on it. The bell probably cost fifty cents, but they had spent days looking for it.

After Hermas died in 1908, Lilly had a terrible time making a living and raising nine kids. I suppose her father and mother helped

Blanchard's grandmother Anna Tinguely (left) *and his mother Lilly Tinguely Blanchard* (right) *are pictured with the Blanchard children in 1900 in Water Canyon. The children are* (back row, left to right) *Rose, Agnes, and Josephine Mary,* (front row, left to right) *Katherine, Arthur, and Edward. The oldest, Charles, is not pictured, and the youngest, Paul, was not yet born.* Courtesy Richard Prince

with a little money over the years, but they were getting old. I know that the Kellys helped raise all those kids. Lilly stayed in Water Canyon until most of the kids were pretty well grown. The year after Hermas died, she and Charlie, who was nineteen and the oldest boy, signed a note at the Ranch Supply Company and mortgaged fifty cows for $497. There were no jobs, and money was hard to come by. During this time, Charlie worked for the Kellys.

The Kellys taught the Blanchard boys to be cowboys—the ones they could teach, that is. Charlie wouldn't ride a horse much, so he never made a cowboy. My dad was ten years older than Ed. My father's youngest brother, Jim Kelly, was born in 1896, so he was two years younger than Ed. As a kid, Uncle Jim was a holy terror—a lot worse than Ed. He could think of all the little tricks to pull. My grandparents had quite a time raising Jim and Ed together. They finally turned them over to my dad and his older brother, who was six years older than my father. From the time Ed and Uncle Jim were small, they were into everything and always in trouble.

My dad and his brother pretty much raised Ed, but they couldn't do much with Charlie. Charlie was too old, and Charlie didn't want to be a cowboy. He wanted to be a miner. But they made a cowboy out of Ed. Ed stayed with the Kellys until 1923, when he drifted away and began to work on other ranches.

When Ed and Uncle Jim were kids, Jim was the leader of the two of them, even though he was the younger one. Ed never did say much, and he didn't have much of a sense of humor even then. My dad told the story of the time when Ed was seven and Jim was five, and Pop and his two older brothers were staying up on Baldy. The elevation at the top of the mountain is about ten thousand feet. It was six miles horseback from the old Kelly house in Water Canyon to the log cabin at the camp on Baldy. The Kellys ran their cattle up on the mountain in the summertime and stayed at the cabin. Then they moved back down to the old log house in Water Canyon during the winter.

My dad said they had been on Baldy three or four days, and they were coming into the cabin one evening when they saw Ed and Uncle Jim riding two burros. They were coming over the ridge, poking those burros with sharp sticks to keep them moving. From then on, these

Jim Kelly and his brother, Frank (Tom Kelly's father), at the old Kelly place in Water Canyon about 1911. Courtesy Tom Kelly

two kids were around and in the way. So the Kellys included them in the cow work and taught them all the bad habits. They took them on to raise.

The Kellys used the cabin on Baldy mainly for shelter when it rained. Even in my time, we slept outside on the ground. When I was a kid, I

Ed Blanchard, pictured in 1913, learned to be a cowboy from his Kelly relatives in Water Canyon. Courtesy Tom Kelly

remember that we cooked right outside the door in Dutch ovens, since there was no stove in the cabin and there were rats in there.

One year, my dad and I were cutting down the gooseberry bushes that had grown up around the cabin. "Pay attention to what you're doing, and see if you find Steve Garst's false teeth," he said.

Steve Garst had spent the night at the cabin. He put his dentures on a rock by his bed before he went to sleep, and next morning they were gone. A rat had carried them off. We dug up every rat den around there looking for Steve's false teeth and never did find them. Steve had to go home because he couldn't eat.

One time while Ed was living near Yucca, Arizona, he stopped by to visit on his way to El Paso. We were sitting at the house shooting the bull when he noticed an iron bean pot I had. "Where did you get that pot?" he asked.

"It's busted," I said. "It's been frozen."

"Yeah, I know," he said. "That's the bean pot from Baldy. We went off one fall and left it full of water. It froze and broke the bottom out of it."

A lot of things happened up on Baldy. About 1910, my dad captured two bear cubs up there. After one of them was almost grown, he traded him to the saloon keeper in Magdalena. The owner kept the bear chained to the rail at the bar. The bear sat on a stool and drank beer like a man. He'd drink until he passed out. That saloon made a lot of money out of that bear. He was a big drawing card. I never heard what happened to the other bear.

There use to be a lot of bears and deer and mountain lions in this country, and nature kept things in balance. There was a fifty-dollar bounty on bears. During the 1920s and 1930s, the state had lion hunters that traveled all over the country, killing them out. Then the state did away with the professional hunters and opened a season on lions. After fifteen years or so, the deer were gone, and what lions were left were starving. The smart lions and bears soon learned to kill calves. They killed half the calf crop every year. The bears even came into the canyon and caught Granny's chickens. But the Kellys took care of their own bear problems.

Back about the time Ed and Jim first showed up on Baldy, Grandpa Kelly had an old yellow hound that was a real good dog, and he would

The Kellys ran their cattle on Mount Baldy during the summers and stayed at their camp there, shown here in 1923. They had a cabin but they slept outside and the cooking was done outside unless the weather was bad. Courtesy Tom Kelly

send him after the horses by himself. That hound often brought those horses in from two miles away. That hound was really valuable to Grandpa Kelly, because he didn't have to go wrangle the horses.

One day my dad and grandfather rode up below the house, and Uncle Jim and Ed had that dog tied down by the creek. They had a fire built and a couple of branding irons were in the fire. My granddad's brand was a double half circle, and damned if those boys hadn't branded his dog! When Grandpa saw that, he had a holy fit. He took after them, but he didn't catch Ed. Ed was bigger and outran him. But he caught Uncle Jim, and I'm sure he broke a couple of sticks on him for branding his dog. That dog was never worth a lot after that. He seemed to be embarrassed that he had that big brand on his side.

Ed and Uncle Jim got around over the country. When I was a kid, every aspen tree in these mountains had their initials on it. Clear back in the early 1900s, EFB or JBK was on everything. All the old cabins around here had one-inch lumber doors that were only five feet high, and Ed's and Jim's initials were on every door all over the mountain. You can still see those initials today.

A few years after Ed and Jim branded ol' Yeller, the dog, they got into trouble again. They must have been ten and twelve years old. A man who lived nearby told them as a joke that Johnny Dobbins had some money buried behind the shed where he lived. Dobbins lived in Water Canyon a little way below the Blanchard house. He had planted little gardens on the flat spots and built rock walls around them. He had a board shed on the hillside. The man told the boys that he had seen ol' Johnny digging a hole to bury his money behind the shed.

One night when Dobbins was gone, Ed and Jim went down there with a pick and shovel. It was a cold, dark night and they couldn't see, so they built a big fire and started digging. The shed caught fire and burned down. The boys left there in a hurry. Needless to say, Dobbins found out who did it, and he didn't see any humor in the situation.

Johnny Dobbins was a fellow who didn't seem to get along with anyone who lived in Water Canyon. He fought with everyone. He had himself appointed justice of the peace, and he was always trying to arrest someone, or he'd file charges against them in Socorro. Then they'd have to go down the canyon to the Water Canyon Station on the Flat and catch the train and go to Socorro for a hearing. He was a real nuisance.

One day after his shed burned, he spotted Jim and Ed, and he grabbed them by the collars and marched them down to the train. He took them to Socorro and put them in jail. In a couple of days when Grandpa Kelly couldn't find the kids, he got to nosing around and found out they were in the Socorro jail. He went to Socorro. He was a little hostile about it, but he paid Dobbins for his shed. Now the kids were really mad at ol' Johnny. They just bided their time.

It wasn't long before Ed and Jim were riding down the canyon toward the Flat, and there was ol' Johnny Dobbins stumbling off down the road to catch the train. They chased him down and roped him and dragged him for a ways. He was pretty scratched up. They rolled him in a ditch and piled a bunch of rocks on him and rode off and left him. They didn't want to kill him; they wanted to teach him a lesson.

My dad was in Socorro, and here came Dobbins. Ol' Johnny wasn't well known for taking baths, and he looked worse than usual. He had been crying, and he was all scratched up and extra dirty. My dad saw him in the courthouse and found out that Johnny was going to file charges against Ed and Jim for trying to murder him. My dad made him believe that that was not a good idea, so Dobbins didn't get them that time. But from then on until Johnny died, he definitely stepped lightly when he knew they were around.

I guess Johnny Dobbins was kind of an exceptional character, because Pop had a lot of stories about him.

Back about the time the Kellys first came to Water Canyon, some bachelors from Germany also settled there. Those Germans built many rock walls in the canyon, and some of them are still there. My dad said one morning years after the shed incident, he and some other men were going up the creek horseback. Johnny had his Model T Ford sitting up on two of these rock walls that were about two feet high, and he was cussing and cranking. The damned thing started and ran over Johnny and jumped off of the rock walls. It ran across the road to a walnut tree. The tree was pretty small, and the car centered that tree and climbed right up it until all that touched the ground were the rear wheels and the bumper. Ol' Johnny had to hire a man with a team to pull his old car out of the tree. Pop always told us this story when we went by this walnut tree.

My dad was away when Dobbins died sometime in the 1920s. Steve Garst, the forest ranger, told Pop about Johnny's funeral one time when I was just a kid. All these old guys who died up here were hauled to Socorro and buried. Steve said they found ol' Johnny up in his house dead. They looked around and found an old suit of clothes in the house, so they decided to clean Johnny up and dress him real pretty and take him to Socorro. He was filthy dirty as ever, so they decided to give him a bath.

Someone had an old long tub they used to scald pigs. They pulled it down to his house and built a big fire under it in the yard to heat the water. They undressed Johnny and plunked him in the tub of water to soak for a while. They were standing nearby talking, and when they looked around, the water was getting pretty hot.

"We damn near gave him too good of a bath," Garst said. "He was just beginning to peel when we pulled him out of there! Johnny hadn't been so clean since he was born. He was the shiniest thing. We dressed him up real pretty and took him to Socorro and had a hell of a funeral! Ol' Johnny would have liked it."

Years before Johnny Dobbins died, Billy Smyth was an old guy who was a bachelor and had a bunch of mining claims in the area. He lived up on a flat in the mouth of Copper Canyon. He had dug a ditch from the creek so he could water his field of alfalfa and his fruit trees. He had a little house on a rock foundation. His mining claims were back around in the hills. He worked some of his claims, and he had one that was pretty good.

During the flu epidemic, Billy got the flu and was pretty sick. He laid up in his two-room board shack and everybody was going up there doctoring on Billy Smyth. My dad went up there one night horseback, and he saw ol' Dobbins and Billy Cozzine, another old guy who lived up the creek. Dobbins and Cozzine were pretty good friends until they got to squabbling over something.

Billy and Johnny were carrying a rusty bucket with an old wooden spoon sticking out of it. "What in the hell you got in the bucket?" my dad asked.

"It's medicine," Dobbins said. "We're going up to Billy's."

"What are you going to do?"

"We're gonna doctor him, and I'll guarantee, we'll either kill him or cure him!"

They had mixed up kerosene and ashes and who knows what else. It was a sloppy-looking mess. Pop just rode on.

Next morning, my dad came down the creek and ol' Johnny was sitting out there. Pop stopped and asked, "How's Billy Smyth doing this morning?"

"He's doing just fine. Our medicine worked!"

"You mean he's cured?"

"Hell, no. It killed him. He was dead this morning, so everything's all right."

They dressed ol' Smyth up and put him on the train and took him to Socorro.

A lot of characters lived in Water Canyon. Some of them were Civil War veterans. Some were Southerners and some were Northerners. They seemed to get along most of the time.

There was one family who moved to Water Canyon about 1900, and the man was in the mining business. The rumor was that he came from a wealthy family in New York, and his wife was said to be from "society." My dad told the story that when they came out West, they were going through a ranch in their buggy. They stopped at this little ranch house because the wife wanted a drink of water. This cowboy got a cup and took her a drink. She threw it in his face and said, "I don't drink from a tin cup!" I imagine that she hated living out here.

The family apparently had money and built quite a settlement near their house. They had a boy who was about my dad's age. His name was Hezekiah, but the kids called him Hezzie. His mother was mortified. She'd say, "His name is NOT Hezzie—It's Hezekiah!"

She often played the piano and sang. My dad and Uncle Bill and Hezzie sat on the hill and listened to her. Pop said it sounded like a whole bunch of howling coyotes. The boys sat up there and mimicked her.

Ol' Hez went to grade school with my dad down at the little school in Water Canyon. Then they had to go to Socorro to high school. Some families moved to Socorro, and others sent their kids there to stay with friends or family during school. Lilly Blanchard had a house in Socorro that Grandpa Tinguely gave her, so the Blanchard kids stayed there.

Hermas never got along too good with Hez's father. For that matter, neither did the Kellys. The Blanchards really got crossways with this guy, especially after Hermas died. I never heard or knew much about this family, but nobody seemed to like the old man.

My dad told me that one time when he was about ten years old, he and his brother, George, who was nineteen years old, were working on the road that ran through the canyon, and all they had was a pick, a shovel, and a hammer. They got thirsty and went down to the creek to get a drink. While they were there, they heard a wagon go up the road. They went back to the road to go back to work and all their tools were gone. They chased the wagon up the road, and Hez's father had their tools in the back of his wagon.

George was the oldest Kelly boy. He grabbed the man out of the wagon and threw him on the ground and kicked him. The man jumped up and took off through the trees, and George couldn't catch him again, but the boys got their tools back. That wasn't the only time that man had sticky fingers.

When Hermas died, the Blanchards went off to Kelly for the funeral. They were gone several days, so they turned the calves out with the milk cows. When they came back, they discovered one of the cows was gone. They got the Kellys to help them hunt for the milk cow, but no one could find her.

Several days later, some of the Blanchards were coming down the trail by this man's house and looked over in his corral and there was their cow's head. They recognized her horns. The man had buried her head in his corral and his dogs had dug it up. The Blanchards got to following tracks around the hill, and they led to a mine shaft. They looked down the shaft, and there was a gunnysack hanging on a nail about twenty feet down. The man had put the hide in a sack and thrown it down the shaft. The boys climbed down and got the sack. Sure enough, there was the milk cow's hide with a Rafter R brand on it. So for several years, it was "get even" time. In those days, you didn't take a man's cow without paying for it one way or another.

Uncle Jim and Ed were about sixteen and eighteen years old. They were going down the canyon road horseback, and they came up on this same guy's wagon with a load of mining equipment. The wagon had a broken wheel, and the man had gone for help. The boys thought they'd give him a little more trouble. They decided they'd play a big trick on him, so they packed all the equipment off his wagon up the hillside and hid it around in the trees. He'd have to do a lot of work to gather it all up. They also found a two-hundred-foot roll of one-and-a-quarter-inch rope. They thought this would be handy, so they just took it with them down to the Flat where the other Kelly Ranch was, and Ed put it under his mattress in the bunkhouse.

A couple of days later the old man showed up, and he was madder than hell. He had found all his equipment except the rope, but he knew who had scattered it around. It didn't take much to figure that out. He got the sheriff, and they had a big search party for this rope. The rope wasn't that valuable, but just like Johnny Dobbins, this guy was always trying to get someone arrested. He was always filing charges against somebody.

The sheriff and this man and a couple of others came to the Flat. No one was there, and they searched the Kellys' board shack and found the rope under the mattress. The man had Uncle Jim and Ed arrested and put in jail. Once again, Grandpa Kelly had to go to Socorro and get them out of jail. They were charged with theft, and the judge had set a court date. They were to go to court over this rope. I don't know what two hundred feet of rope was worth then, but this man was prosecuting it for all he could.

Before the case came to trial, Grandpa Kelly decided he had to find two hundred feet of that rope somewhere and buy it. He learned that the rope had come from Montgomery Ward. The rope had a red thread woven through the center of each strand, and there was no way in the world he could come up with two hundred feet of rope like that with a bill dated back before Ed and Uncle Jim had taken it from this man. He looked all over the country trying to find some.

One morning Steve Garst rode up from the ranger station down the canyon. "I know where there's a whole coil of that same rope," Steve told Grandpa Kelly. "I'll go get you two hundred feet of it."

So Steve left Water Canyon one morning and rode thirty miles to Riley. He took a packhorse and brought back two hundred feet of that rope with a red thread through it. Steve had a bill from that store dated back about a month before the boys had acquired the rope, so there was no case against Ed and Jim.

Several years after that, Garst was still living down at the ranger station. This same man had a lot of hogs running loose up and down the canyon. He had pigs everywhere. They were in everyone's way. They busted into barns and sheds and ate the grain and tore up the alfalfa bales.

Steve left the door of his big barn open one day, and a sow that belonged to this man got in there and tore up five hundred pounds of grain. Garst was madder than hell, so he just ran her down in the creek and killed her. He butchered her and skinned her out. The guy was always snooping up and down the canyon, and he found the hog hanging out there with his earmark on it, so he had the forest ranger arrested.

After Steve got out of trouble, he rode up to the Kelly house. He needed some help and the Kellys owed him a debt. They held a war

[55]

conference and decided to fix the guy once and for all. It wasn't the last time they had to deal with him, however.

The Kellys had four or five old sows running around, too. So they caught their hogs and put the same earmark on them that the old man's had. When they got to court, Grandpa Kelly got up and swore he had given Steve a hog, and it was that hog Steve had killed. That got Steve out of his predicament. Everyone was happy except the guy who lost the hog.

This man was a real winner. Everyone in the area seemed to hate him. I can remember him when I was a little kid. By that time, he had palsy real bad, and he shook all the time. This was 1928 or 1929. He was talking to my dad one day. I later asked who he was, because he looked sick.

"Yeah, and I hope the son-of-a-bitch lives another fifty years just like that!" my dad said.

In his later years, this man survived on making bootleg whiskey. He had a lot of fruit trees, and my dad said he made peach brandy and apricot brandy. He'd put two gallons over the front of his saddle and ride down to the station. He'd tie his horse and catch the train to Magdalena and sell his brandy. He didn't have a dime when he died in Magdalena, but he had 240 acres that he left to Hez's wife. He didn't leave anything to his son.

There was another good bootlegger and cow thief who came by the Kelly Ranch on the Flat one time. He had four kegs of moonshine to sell in Magdalena, but he stopped at the ranch to spend the night with Pop. He had two mules with a keg on each side of each mule. He had a bottle of hooch and he passed it around for all to have a drink.

Next morning before he went to Magdalena to make arrangements to sell his whiskey, he led his mules up in the mountains and buried his kegs. Ed Blanchard saw him, and when he left, Ed dug up a keg. Pop said it sure was smooth.

Ed finally grew up. He stayed in the Water Canyon area until 1918, when he was drafted into the army during World War I. By that time, he had become a pretty wild cowboy. He stayed with the Kellys in the old cabin on Baldy and helped them with their cattle. I don't think he got paid for working, but he learned the occupation.

Ed Blanchard in Water Canyon in 1918. Courtesy Tom Kelly

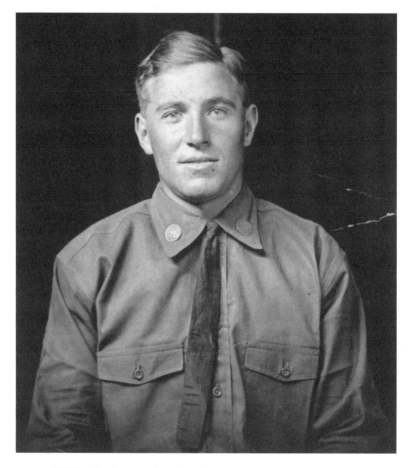

Ed Blanchard in 1918 while in the U.S. Army during World War I.
Courtesy Tom Kelly

Then, of course, he had his mother's cows to take care of, too, and they were half wild. They ran at the head of a big canyon that was full of rock slides and steep hillsides and trees. Ed learned to be a holy terror on a horse. He was probably the wildest cowboy you could ever find. He never cared where the horse went or how fast he was going or how steep the hill was or if there were trees in the way. What he couldn't go through or over, he tore down, which often got him knocked off of his horse. He was a complete idiot when he got after a wild cow.

[58]

One time my dad and I were up in the canyon. Someone was digging a prospect hole on the hillside with a Caterpillar tractor. They had gone off the hill and broken some limbs off of a tree. My dad stopped and looked at the tree. "If I didn't know better," he said, "I'd swear Ed Blanchard went off through there!"

When Ed got after a cow, he pulled his hat down over his eyes, ducked his head, and took off. Whatever got in the way, he either broke off or went under or over. He was hurt many times, but that's the kind of cowboy he was—about half crazy. He'd rope a cow anywhere. He didn't care if it was on top of the bluff or if she had jumped off the bluff—he still tried to rope her.

I asked Ed's cousin, Billy Cook, who was raised around him, if Ed was a good roper. "If you've got a fifty-foot rope and a loop as big as this room, when you throw it out there, you're bound to catch something!" he said.

In those days, if a cowboy caught a cow around the belly, it was just fine. If he caught one by the head, it was okay. If he caught an old wild cow by the front leg or the hind leg, then the wrestling match was on. So that's the kind of cowboy that Ed Blanchard learned to be.

CHAPTER 4

From Horseback
to Horsepower

Ed Blanchard, Jim Kelly, and Fred Martin were iducted into the army at the same time. They reported to Camp Cody at Deming, New Mexico, on April 11, 1918. The army was buying horses all over the country to be used in World War I. Some of them were six- and seven-year-olds that had never been broke, so the boys were in their element when they were sent to Fort Sam Houston in San Antonio, Texas, to break horses. Everything was a big joke to them, and more than likely, they broke all the horses to buck so they could get even with the cavalry. When they weren't shoveling manure for doing something wrong, they were breaking horses. They spent about a year in the army before the war ended. Ed was discharged at Camp Travis on January 21, 1919, and came back to the Kelly Ranch in New Mexico.

Ed had ridden horses all of his life, so that was his expertise. He always helped the Kellys break their horses. Each year, they handled them for the first time up on Baldy. They ran them into the corral and tied them down. Each man took a horse and saddled him and then rode him off of the mountain. That made for some wild rides!

When Ed and Uncle Jim were young and they didn't think they had enough ornery horses of their own to ride, they would go down the Rio Grande and steal ten to fifteen little Mexican horses and bring them up to Water Canyon to practice on for fun. As I said earlier—they weren't angels.

My dad recalled a horse deal that he and Grandpa Kelly made one time with Al Clements, who had a horse ranch on the north end of the San Mateo Mountains. Clements had several hundred horses that had never been touched, and he wanted Pop, Uncle Jim, and Ed to break them.

They gathered seventy-five of these horses—all stallions that had never been branded or handled—and brought them to the Flat to break. The deal was that for breaking them, the Kellys could take their pick of half the horses and return the other half to Clements. Pop said they were all so mean they could hardly do anything with them. After they got them half broke, Clements got the bucking part back. If there were any good horses, the Kellys kept them. Pop said

Ed Blanchard, Frank Kelly, and Jim Kelly (left to right) *had their photo made at the Ranger Station in Water Canyon in 1918 before they left to join the army during World War I.* Courtesy Tom Kelly

[61]

that's where Ed really learned to be a bronc rider. Every one of those horses bucked.

Ed was only five feet, five inches tall, but he was husky and strong. The boys ran a big, six-year-old horse into the corral, roped him and blindfolded him, and Ed cinched his saddle on him. He had trouble reaching the stirrup, so he jumped up and caught it with the toe of his boot so he could climb in the saddle. That started the wreck!

That ol' horse shot off and the blindfold came off and around and around the corral he went. He threw Ed up on his neck. Then he threw him behind the saddle—then back to his neck again. This time the buttons on the front of Ed's pants caught over the saddle horn, and ol' Ed was up on that horn spinning around and around in a circle, flattened out on top of that bucking horse. Finally, Ed's pants tore off of him, and he landed out on the ground. They thought he had been killed.

Uncle Jim ran out to Ed and shook him, and Ed finally mumbled something and staggered to his feet. He held his head and sidled over against the fence until he got his senses back. They caught the horse, and Ed went out there and climbed back on again. He was determined to ride that horse, and he did. Ed was so hard-headed, you couldn't tell him no about anything he wanted to do. If he listened to anyone, it was my dad's sister Mable.

Mable and her husband, Tally Cook, had the Currycomb Ranch southwest of Water Canyon. The ranch headquarters was about ten miles up the Alamosa River north of Monticello. Ed always hung around Aunt Mable when he could. I guess she was his favorite. Anytime he didn't have a job, he went to the Cooks' and stayed with them. He lived in the log bunkhouse behind the ranch house. I suppose they paid him wages off and on, so he had work and made a little money.

Tally Cook had come to New Mexico from Texas. He worked for the Santa Fe Railway, and he had been in New Mexico for some time when he first met Mable. Uncle Tally, Hal Gage, and Albert Woofter all worked for the railroad. Ol' man Woofter was an engineer. They all were fired at the same time for letting hobos ride the trains. Woofter left New Mexico in 1917 and went to Texas and became a drilling

When Blanchard worked for the Currycomb Ranch, he lived in this log bunkhouse behind the main house. Photo by Jane Pattie

contractor in the oil fields around Mexia and Wortham. While he was still in Texas in 1921, he bought a large ranch thirty miles from Magdalena and finally settled on it permanently in 1927. He became one of the most successful cattlemen in Socorro County.

Tally and a partner bought the seventy-five-section Currycomb Ranch on the Alamosa River in 1914. They sold some cattle one year, and the partner left with the money. Tally went to Texas to work in the oil fields in order to make the payments on his ranch. I've never heard it said that he worked for Woofter, but it seems likely.

My dad said Tally was just freshly married to his sister, Mable, when he came down to the Flat one time to help the Kellys gather cattle. It was about 1913. They had a bunch of horses in the corral, and they roped one for Tally. The horse had bucked every once in a while, as most of them had. Tally stepped up on him, and that horse broke in two and bucked all over the corral.

"By G__! That man could ride a horse!" my dad said. "He sure did surprise us!"

I think Uncle Tally had been set up, but he had the last laugh. He was no greenhorn.

I don't know when Ed Blanchard first began staying down at the Cooks', but he considered them family. In those days, to get to the Currycomb from the Kelly Ranch, you took a packhorse and went horseback over the top of Mount Baldy, down across Milligan Gulch, and over the San Mateos. When you got to the other side, you were at the Cooks' ranch. It was about a two-day ride. That's the way Ed went back and forth from Water Canyon.

Ed worked for the Kellys until about 1923, when he figured he was good enough to be a cowboy anywhere. He began working around at ranches all over the country. He did that from 1923 until he moved to Arizona and finally made spurs full time. But he wasn't thinking of spurs during those early days when he went to the Cooks'. They had a cabin on top of the mountain, and they had wild cows. That was heaven to Ed Blanchard.

Aunt Mable and Uncle Tally had three boys—Bob, the oldest, Porter, and Billy, the little guy. They were pretty much raised around Ed Blanchard. Ed would go there and often stay six months at a time. Then he'd get mad about something and take off and go to another ranch and work for a year or two. When he lost that job, he'd go back to Aunt Mable's.

Ed was staying at the Cooks' in about 1923 when he loaded Aunt Mable and the kids into a wagon and took them downriver to pick apples. Aunt Mable wanted to make jelly, and there were some old orchards two or three miles down the canyon that had been abandoned years before, but the trees still had fruit. The river stayed flooded all summer and was six hundred yards or more wide. Every time the water got up, the road along the creek washed out and left piles of rocks, old logs and trees, and big holes. It could be rough-going in a wagon.

Ed went out to harness the team and hook them to the wagon. I'm sure Uncle Tally had gentle work horses, but Ed decided it was a good time to break a wild mule to harness. He hooked up the wild mule alongside a gentle mule and loaded the two oldest boys, who were about six and eight, into the back of the wagon. Mable climbed up on the seat beside Ed and held little Billy, the youngest of the bunch. Ed flicked the reins and away they went at top speed down this river full of rocks, washouts, and logs. The wild mule tried to run off and the other one tried to hold him back. All the time Ed was dodging pitfalls, and Mable was hollering at Bob and Porter to hang on. She called Ed Blanchard a nitwit and yelled for him to slow down. But he didn't have much control of the mules' speed.

Ed had hold of the lines and was sawing away with the bits in an attempt to slow the runaways when the wagon hit a deep wash. Ed did a somersault over the dashboard of the wagon and landed upside down with one spur hung in the brake stick and the other one on the dashboard. He had lost one line, but he had a death grip on the other, which caused the mules to go around and around in a big circle. Ed was still hanging upside down over the front of the wagon. Mable screamed that they had lost the kids out of the wagon and might run over them. She was hanging onto Billy and probably calling Ed worse names than nitwit. Ed finally managed to crawl back up onto the seat, and he got hold of the other line and stopped the team. The mules were pretty well winded by then.

They hadn't lost Bob and Porter after all. They were still in the back of the wagon, but they were big-eyed after that ride. The only one who wasn't upset was Ed Blanchard. It was all in a day's work. He got his mules in hand and headed on to the orchard. They picked their fruit, but Mable didn't have much to say to Ed. They even made it back to the ranch that evening without bruising any of the apples they'd gathered.

Ed stepped around pretty lightly for a week or so. It took Mable that long to get in a good humor again, but I don't think Ed Blanchard took them for any more wagon rides for a while. In fact, he might have moved on to cowboy at another ranch while the air cleared.

From this time on, Ed worked on various ranches. He worked for Dub Evans at the Slashes Ranch down on the Gila River. He also worked for H. C. Badger and Hal Bruner, who had the Muleshoe Ranch west of the Magdalena Mountains and the Diamond Bar on the Gila. Ed worked for the W Bars and on a ranch at Bear Springs that had a lot of country north of Magdalena. He worked for the C Bar N out on the San Agustin Plain and for the Jeffers Ranch, and he was down at Fred Martin's. Ed worked on about every ranch in this country.

Blanchard's cousins, the Cook boys. Left to right: *Porter on Miller, Billy on Clavelli, and Bob on Solis at the Currycomb Ranch.* Courtesy Bill Cook

In those days, a cowboy had his own special gear. He had an old saddle that just fit him, and it usually had taps on the stirrups. He had his camp gear and bedroll and, of course, his chaps, boots, spurs, hat, rope, and his own horses.

Ed's horses were something out of this world. He liked the orneriest horse he could find. There was something the matter with every horse he ever had. It would either buck and try to throw Ed off every time he got on him, or it would rear up and fall over backward. That was the horse Ed always bragged on. He broke a lot of horses in his younger days, and he rode many different horses over the years. I'm sure he rode some good ones as well as bad ones, but the ones I remember were all pretty rank. Ed was riding one of those half-broke broncs the day he tied the dynamite behind his saddle.

The Cook boys were always leery of dynamite after Porter had lost three fingers while playing with dynamite caps when he was a small child. He had found a little red can stuck up under the water tank. It looked like a nice little toy. It had a couple of dynamite caps in it, and when he shook it, they exploded and mangled his fingers.

One morning after the boys were almost grown, they were going to ride up in the mountains with Ed and do some work. In the area where they were headed, Ed had been digging around in a little wet spot that appeared to be a spring. As they saddled up to leave the Currycomb headquarters, Ed came out of a barn with three sticks of dynamite and shoved them in his coat, which was tied on the back of his saddle. He planned to use the dynamite to bring in a water well.

"Wait a minute," he said. "I almost left the caps and a fuse." He again disappeared into a shed and came out with a small tin can and stuck it up into his coat with the dynamite.

Dynamite is dangerous if it's old or it's been frozen or gotten hot. It can go off with the slightest jar, and of course, the caps were what had gotten Porter's fingers. A prudent man would not carry the two together, but no one ever said Ed Blanchard was prudent.

Ed had saddled a spooky horse, and he led it out in the open space below the corral. He tried to get on him, but the horse squirmed and jumped around. Ed's way of quieting him down was to pull the horse's head around and kick him in the belly. Then he tried again to climb up on the horse. When all this started, the Cooks began putting a little distance between themselves and Ed, because they were expecting a terrible big bang. They all headed for cover.

Ed finally got his leg over the saddle, but the horse had such a fit trying to buck that he reared up and fell over backward. When there was no loud explosion, the Cooks peeked out to see what was happening. Ed and the horse were both still in one piece and there was no five-foot hole in the ground. Ed was kicking at the horse to get him up. He got into the saddle as the horse got to his feet.

"Let's go!" he hollered at the Cooks. "Or are you gonna stand around here all day gazing at the stars?"

After all this excitement, they figured they'd have to ride three hundred yards behind Ed all the way. It looked like it was too explosive a situation for them. They told him to just go on, and they'd catch up with him later. I guess he didn't blow up, since he made lots of spurs after that. Being around Ed Blanchard could be plumb dangerous.

[67]

• • •

Uncle Tally Cook was broke in 1926 and 1927. He had a payment due on the ranch, and that's when he went to Texas to work in the oil fields. He took his whole family and left Ed Blanchard to run the Currycomb while he was gone.

When the Cooks came back two years later, Ed hadn't done much. None of the calves had been branded, and Ed wasn't there. He came in the next day with a herd of ranch horses. He had had most of the horses out in the Black Range, where he had been for quite a while helping the Pankeys gather a remnant of wild cattle off the Ladder Ranch, northwest of Hillsboro. Ed was so wild on a horse that he had crippled most of the Cooks' horses. There wasn't one of them hardly fit to ride. Uncle Tally wasn't very happy.

The Pankeys used a couple of pretty good cow dogs in this wild-cow gathering. Ed never did like dogs, and these dogs hated ol' Ed, but the Pankeys got pretty good use out of their dogs. Every time Ed got close to one of the dogs, he hollered at it or cussed it out. According to Ed and his brother Charlie, anything they disliked was "sickening." One night in camp, Bill Pankey told him, "Ed, if you'd be a little better to those dogs, they'd help you."

"Those sickening damned things aren't any good," Ed grumbled. "Every time I get close to them, they just flop over and lay there until I get out of sight."

"If you'd just throw them a biscuit every now and then, they'd become your friends and they'd help you."

Ed just glowered and walked off. "I don't want the sons-of-bitches around my bed." He kicked at one to get him out of the way. Needless to say, Ed never had any luck with the dogs.

When Ed got back to the Currycomb with all these worn-out crippled horses, no one had a horse to ride. They were afoot. Cook had other horses back up the Alamosa River, so the next morning, Uncle Tally told Ed to go up the river and bring the horses out of the horse pasture to the house. Ed talked Bob, the oldest Cook boy, into helping gather these horses.

One of the horses in the herd was a gentle mare that was Ed's. He and Bob Cook were running the horses down the Alamosa toward the house. Ed was up on a little bank, and the mare was down in the creek. Ed threw his rope at her and caught her. When the mare hit the end of the rope, she jerked Ed's horse off of the bank, and the horse and Ed fell down in the creek. The horse got up and walked away, but Ed lay there with a bone sticking out of his leg. They were two miles from headquarters.

Bob hurried on to the house for help. Uncle Tally was gone, so Aunt Mable put a mattress in the Model T truck, drove up the river to Ed, and got him down to the house. He was really suffering. The Cooks had a Mexican man who worked around headquarters, and Mable sent him in the car to Hot Springs, which is now Truth or Consequences, to get Dr. White. This all happened pretty early in the day, but the doctor didn't get there until after dark, and Ed was really hurting.

The doctor set the leg and put a cast on it. He said it might work. As he was setting Ed's leg, he raved about what beautiful country he crossed coming to the ranch. Come to find out, the doctor had his camera with him, and he stopped to take pictures along the way. He said he was afraid it might be dark on his way back. That's why it had taken him so long to get there.

He told Ed to stay in bed and off of his leg, but Ed would get up and "cripple" outside to the outhouse. Ed was so nasty-nice that he wouldn't use the slop jar in the house. While walking on this broken leg, something happened to it. When Uncle Tally arrived back at home two weeks later, Ed was really sick and his leg was badly swollen.

Tally loaded him in the car and took him to the Veterans Hospital in Albuquerque. Ed had an infection that affected many of the bones in his body. He was in the hospital for six months. They even cut out some of his ribs. He may have had some ribs broken when the horse fell on him. When Ed was released from the hospital, he went back to the Currycomb. He had scars all over him. He crippled around and said he was ready to go back to work, but he could barely walk. Uncle Tally made him rest for two weeks.

Ed soon had rested about all he could stand. Perhaps he had a twinge of conscience, though, because Tally Cook had four or five half-Percheron three-year-old horses Ed was supposed to have broken while the Cooks were in Texas, and he hadn't ridden a one of them. Ed was ready to go break those horses. The Cooks said he couldn't do it—he was too crippled. That's all it took. Ed bowed his neck and said, "By G__, I can!" He said he needed the wages if Tally was still willing to pay him.

"If you think you're able, go do it!" Tally finally told him.

The first horse he caught was a big, strong son-of-a-gun that had never had a rope on him. Ed roped him around the neck and then got dragged all over the corral. Finally, all the Cook boys got on the rope and got the horse down and put a hackamore on him. They blindfolded him and cinched Ed's saddle on him. Ol' Ed sacked him out a little and said, "He's ready. I guess I'll get on him."

The horse was so tall that Ed had to jump to reach the stirrup. When he jumped, the horse went to bucking, and he threw Ed about twenty-five feet in the air. He landed out in the middle of the corral and just lay there. The boys thought they had killed him. They ran out and got him over to the fence. He sat there until he got his marbles together.

Ed Blanchard wasn't a quitter. "By G__, I'm gonna ride that horse!" he swore.

He got back on him, and the horse threw him again. This happened three times. By the third time, Ed was beginning to wonder where in the hell he was. The kids got the horse down and took the saddle and hackamore off and turned him loose. Ed hobbled back to the house and said that if he couldn't ride that horse, no one could.

Tally told Ed not to get on him anymore. He would make a work horse out of him, and that's what he did. Ed went ahead and broke the others over a period of time.

Ed was so hard-headed you couldn't tell him anything. He liked those mean horses. In fact, if he had a gentle horse, he'd try to make it mean or crazy. He thought if he was working for an outfit and he had a couple of real good gentle horses, they'd take them away from him and give them to somebody else. If he kept them ornery, no one else would want to ride them. That's why his horses were so mean.

By 1930, Ed had ridden a lot of broncs and chased many a wild cow. He could also steal a cow or two every once in a while if he had to. But in those days, people were different. If someone stole a cow from a man, he would usually steal two or three back to get even. Ed acquired extra cattle that way, too, and must have made a little money doing this in his younger days.

Ed was staying with the Cooks at the Currycomb in 1929. He had acquired some money, and I guess he thought he was rich. He decided to buy a car. There was a Ford agency in Magdalena, and Ed liked the looks of a pretty little roadster and decided to buy it. He had never driven a car, but I guess he had ridden in one once.

Milt, the owner of the agency, got in the car with Ed and took him up one street and down another. He showed him how you turned the wheel and where the clutch and the brakes were. By the time they got back to the Ford agency, Ed was an expert driver, because Milt had showed him how to do it.

Bob Cook was about fourteen years old then, and he went to school in Magdalena. It was the beginning of a school vacation, so Ed went by and picked Bob up. Bob was just a kid, but he could drive. Ed and Bob headed for the Currycomb, about sixty miles by dirt road. Ed had Bob drive until they got out of town, and then Ed took over. After all, he was an expert driver. He tore up half the bushes between Magdalena and the ranch. The bottom of the car was soon pretty well polished by rocks and bushes and everything Ed had run over.

By the time Ed and Bob got to the Currycomb, Bob was getting a little wild.

Tally Cook and Bob's brother, Porter, were standing out by the corral. They heard the roadster coming down the river before they saw it. The Alamosa is about ten feet wide and a foot deep in water where it runs past headquarters. The house sits on a little rise facing the river, and the corral is across an open area to the side of the house. Tally and Porter saw this fancy new car coming around the bend across the river, but they had no idea who it could be.

As Ed turned across the Alamosa toward the corral, Bob yelled, "Give her hell, Ed! Give her hell, or you'll never make the hill!" Ed gave her the gun.

He had the roadster in second gear. They flew across that river, and it looked like the car had wings. Water sprayed up about fifty feet high on each side and danged near covered everything up. They came roaring up that little rise, and about that time Uncle Tally realized who it was.

"Damn! That's just what we need to finish this place off," Uncle Tally mumbled. "Ed Blanchard in a car!"

The roadster shot across the clearing and was headed straight for the corral when Bob grabbed the wheel and turned it. The car made a circle in the big open area, and Ed was still giving it the gas. They made a couple of rounds and headed toward the house. The car's emergency brake was on the floor by the gearshift. Bob reached down and jerked on the brake, and the roadster slid to a stop. The car chugged a little and died.

Ed turned to Bob. "Well, gee whiz, Bob—what did you stop here for? I didn't want to park here."

By now, all the Cooks had figured out that here was Ed Blanchard in a brand new 1929 Model A roadster. He was really in the chips! He was ready to start chasing the girls now.

Ed was always a little scared of women. I never knew him to be too friendly toward any woman. He shied away from all of them. But he got his nerve up and made about three trips to Hot Springs to chase the girls. He was going to get him a girlfriend with this new car.

He stopped at a neighboring ranch and picked up another cowboy, and they headed to Hot Springs to get dates. But Ed never had much luck. This cowboy told Billy Cook that Ed thought women were like wild cows. He just threw a hammerlock on one and wallowed her around, and the gal would run off and go home. That pretty much cured Ed of his woman-chasing days.

Maybe it went back to the way he was reared with all the girls in the family and four boys. It was always a big joke in the outfit that when the mother and girls washed their "under drawers," as they called them, the boys never could be around. When they hung the underclothes out on the line to dry, they always hung them in pillowcases, so the boys couldn't see them. Who knows—maybe this affected ol' Ed in his later life.

It must have affected Charlie, too. He was older than Ed, but Charlie never had anything to do with women in the eighty-something years he lived. He always called them "sickening damn women." As I've said, everything was "sickening" that they didn't like. It was a "sickening damn horse" or a "sickening damn cow." Ed and Charlie were different from the rest of the family. Some of the girls were married and the two younger boys left and married and had kids. But Ed and Charlie were different. They were typical old bachelors and set in their ways.

The oldest girl, Mary Josephine, left Water Canyon early, and no one heard from her for forty years. They thought she was dead. She showed up at our house one day looking for the Blanchards, since they had been living in Water Canyon when she left. Of course, they had all left the canyon by then. Pop told her how to find Ed and Charlie.

When Charles Blanchard saw her later in Arizona at Ed's, he started hollering, "It's a ghost! A ghost!" He wouldn't look at her. Charlie was a little peculiar.

The Blanchard family had split up when Lilly became a Holy Roller, as church members of that persuasion were called then. Those were really terrible words in the outfit. I've heard Ed and Charlie cuss the Holy Rollers, as did my side of the family. It was all because of one thing. One of the older Tinguely boys, Charles Albert, who was Ed and Charlie's uncle, married a woman who was a Holy Roller.

When my dad was a kid, he and the other boys peeked in the window one night when the Holy Rollers were having one of their meetings. "The crazy things were running around screaming and falling over on the floor!" Pop said. "By golly, it was dangerous to go there. You might be killed!"

Ed and Charlie thought the same as the Kellys. I don't know what the rest of the Blanchards thought.

Albert Tinguely's wife was around a lot, and she got Lilly interested in the Holy Rollers. But it was Albert who really separated my part of the family from some of the Blanchards and Tinguelys. He had a store south of here in San Marcial. Times got hard, and he wasn't making much money. He had to find a way to get rid of the store, because it was just a drag. According to his brother, Sam Tinguely, Albert gave twenty dollars to a Mexican to burn the store down. He had it insured for five thousand dollars.

Albert headed up to Socorro and was sitting in the Green Front Saloon having a little toddy when the store burned to the ground. Everything he owned went up in flames, and he collected the five thousand dollars.

Everything was glorious. He had the five thousand dollars, but his wife, the Holy Roller, knew he burned the store. She and her preacher turned him in to the insurance company to collect the reward. In

1909, poor ol' Tinguely had to take up residence in the territorial penitentiary in Santa Fe for a couple of years. When he was released on March 25, 1911, he went to El Paso even though the El Paso Tinguelys were Holy Rollers and Albert was a Methodist. Even Charlie Blanchard eventually stayed down in El Paso off and on, but Ed didn't go around them much for quite a while.

However, Ed did go to El Paso when he got his new roadster. He decided to go visit his family for Thanksgiving and show off his car. He had been practicing driving it by going to Hot Springs and probably was doing fairly well on the dirt roads. He got to El Paso and finally found where his mother lived. He wasn't gone but four days when he showed back up at the Currycomb, mad and grouchy. He said he took that new car to El Paso so he could give them all a ride, but no one would get in with him. They didn't have as much nerve as Bob Cook had.

The Currycomb Ranch had a real bear problem in the San Mateo Mountains in the mid-1930s. There were so many that they killed a cow a day. Tally sent Ed and Porter up to stay in the Cooks' cabin on top of the mountain so they could get rid of the bears.

One morning Ed and Porter were going through a bad thicket in the bottom of a little narrow canyon, and they met a big ol' bear face to face. Ed grabbed his .30-30 and shot the bear, but he didn't kill it. The bear ran at them, and Ed's horse reared up and fell over backward. The bear went right over the top of Ed and his horse and left the canyon. They later found him dead. None of this bothered Ed, but it scared Porter out of several days' growth.

The game department sent Emmett Bonnerman up there to hunt bears. He had Lum Woods's pack of dogs. Woods was an old lion and bear hunter and Emmett's father-in-law.

Emmett and Ed hit a fresh bear track one morning, and the dogs took off at a dead run. Of course, Ed stayed with them, making a trail through the scrub trees like a small bulldozer. When the hunter caught up with them, the dogs had the bear up a tree. The bear kept backing down, trying to get away. Ed was running around the tree kicking the bear in the butt, making him go back up. All the time, he was hollering, "Get back up that tree, you s.o.b.!"

I guess ol' Ed was a little tougher than that bear.

Top: *Blanchard made his style No. 4 drop shank and chap guard spur in stainless steel for the Cook brothers with Bill and Porter's brand, the Lazy D Slash, on the outside heel bands.* Courtesy Bill Cook. Second from top: *Blanchard's style No. 5, Bill Simon Cutting Horse Spurs, were popular because they stayed put on a cowboy's boots. Blanchard's heel bands were always one inch to one and a half inches in width, and the spurs were noted for their slanted buttons. These features allowed for a proper fit. They could be ordered in plain or stainless steel, mounted or unmounted.* Courtesy Dale and Mary K Gallaher. Photo by Jane Pattie. Second from bottom: *Typical of the spurs Blanchard made in Yucca, Arizona, style No. 6 spurs were sleek but simple and utilitarian. This pair is marked with the maker's name, location, and No. 6 PS (plain steel). Unmounted spurs such as these were sold by saddle shops and feed stores throughout the west.* Courtesy Dale and Mary K Gallaher. Photo by Jane Pattie. Bottom: *This pair of Blanchard's style No. 8 spur has sawtooth rowels and reflects the contoured button straps typical of his later spurs.* Courtesy Tom Kelly

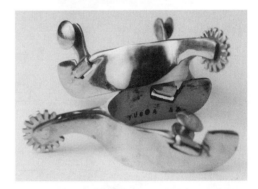

Well-made spurs with chap guards crafted by Hugh Pankey in 1922 or 1923 for his brother, Joe. The Flying X brand is on the outside heel band, and on the inside is a silver quarter moon on either side of a star. The silver mounting is made from Harvey House silverware. The spur bands are not rounded on the ends or cut out for the button straps, and there is very little angle to the swingers. Courtesy Rueben Pankey

Ed made these kid's spurs for Tom Kelly in 1932 or 1933. He met the school bus and gave them to young Tom. They are some of the first spurs Blanchard made. In 1947, he replaced the rowels and re-worked some of the mounting. They are full-mounted with Tom's initials and a silver heart on a copper diamond, plus silver embellishments on the shanks. Unmarked. Courtesy Tom Kelly. Photo © Hoss Fosso, 1999

Unmarked spurs made by Blanchard for Jack Hulse of Magdalena. This early pair of his spurs is hand-forged and of one-piece construction with a narrow shank extending from a wide, flat heel band. The outside mount is Hulse's Double Spade brand. The inside heel band has a silver diamond mount. Blanchard's slanting buttons are set over cut-out slots in the heel bands. There are silver covers over the rowel pins, and copper plates cover the shanks inside and out. Courtesy Bob Fryer. Photo by Mel Gnatkowski

A pair of Blanchard's early-day spurs made in 1933 or 1934 for George Latham, a cowboy who worked for the Pankeys. They are full-mounted, one-piece spurs mounted on the outside heel bands with a silver A Cross brand and silver on the shank and over the rowel pins. On the inside band is a copper diamond. Courtesy Rueben Pankey

It is said that Blanchard made these spurs in the 1940s or earlier for a rancher named Tipton whose land was located twelve miles north of Luna, New Mexico, in Spur Lake Basin. Tipton wore the spurs for thirty years before he gave them to a cowboy friend. They are double-mounted with silver and copper overlays and brass inlays in the outside of the rowel spokes. The buttons are set at a slant, but the heel bands are not cut out behind the button straps as was typical of Blanchard spurs. Unmarked. Courtesy A. C. Cook. Photo by Jane Pattie

Claude "Hump" Humphreys was a good cowboy as well as a top rodeo bronc rider who often worked as an extra in Hollywood Westerns during the rodeo off-season. Blanchard made spurs to order, and this is a rare pair of gal-legs, embellished with silver and brass, and copper garters, made in the late 1930s or early 1940s. The buttons are set at only a slight angle and the heel bands are not cut out behind the button swingers. Unmarked. Courtesy Dale and Mary K Gallaher. Photo by Jane Pattie

Blanchard made this pair of one-piece spurs at the Currycomb Ranch in the 1940s for Magdalena rancher George Foster. Each of their outside slanted buttons is decorated with a copper star. The spurs are double-mounted, overlaid with silver on the outside heel band and brass on the inside and are hand-forged from one piece of steel. The silver plate on the outside heel band is made from a hammered fifty-cent piece, and a brass steer head decorates the opposite heel band. Unmarked. Courtesy Randy Perkins. Photo by Mel Gnatkowski

Blanchard made bits through 1962 until spur orders kept him too busy. Bits were always made to order. Ed would have a cowboy send a drawing of what was wanted and would work from that. Blanchard bits are rare and collectable. Courtesy Tom Kelly. Photo by Jane Pattie

Unmarked spurs made by Blanchard for Bill Pankey in 1942. Courtesy Rueben Pankey

Tom Kelly believes this to be one of a pair of Blanchard's personal spurs. Ed's brand, Rafter R, is stippled on the silver overlay on the base of the shank. This pair is plain steel and of one-piece construction. The button hangers are bradded on at a slight angle. The spurs are double-mounted and embellished with a large silver plate on the outside heel band that is engraved with a spade. The plate on the inside heel band is engraved with a steer head. The rowels have been replaced. Made in the 1940s at Monticello. Unmarked. Courtesy Bob Fryer. Photo by Mel Gnatkowski

These were one-piece spurs when Ed made them for Frank Kelly in 1944. When the rowels and shanks wore out, Tom Kelly sent them to Blanchard, and he cut the shanks off and welded on new ones. He replaced the rowels and the Double Half Circle brands. In 1944, a pair of Blanchard bits and spurs cost $25.00. Ed continued to make this style No. 4 drop shank with chap guard. Courtesy Tom Kelly. Photo © Hoss Fosso, 1999

Two pairs of Blanchard spurs from the collection of Bill Swope, Cherokee, Texas. The spurs on the right were given to Swope by the late Texas Ranger Charlie Miller. They are decorated with a brand and have a flat piece of silver on the outside heel band on which the background is stippled around Miller's initials, which are left smooth. These were probably made at Jim Kelly's ranch on the Flat or in Datil. Blanchard used this style of mounting during the early 1940s. Tom Kelly believes that the pair on the left was sold to a feed store or saddle shop as plain spurs with only a star on the button and later mounted by another spur maker. Neither pair is marked. Photo by Jane Pattie

Ed made this pair of one-piece steel spurs for Jim Kelly, Tom Kelly's brother, in 1946. They are full-mounted, having Jim's initials on one side of the heel bands and the Kelly brand, the Double Half Circle, on the other. Courtesy Tom Kelly. Photo © Hoss Fosso, 1999

[82]

Blanchard made this pair of stainless steel spurs for rancher George Coupland. He began making welded two-piece stainless steel spurs and stamping them in Datil, New Mexico, in 1946 or 1947. This pair is marked E.F.B. inside the heel bands. They are embellished with Coupland's CX brand. This is an early welded spur as is evident from the sharp angle where the shank is attached to the heel band and the blow holes and grinder marks along the weld. The slanted rods for the buttons straps are welded instead of bradded. Courtesy Mike Shivers. Photo by Mel Gnatkowski

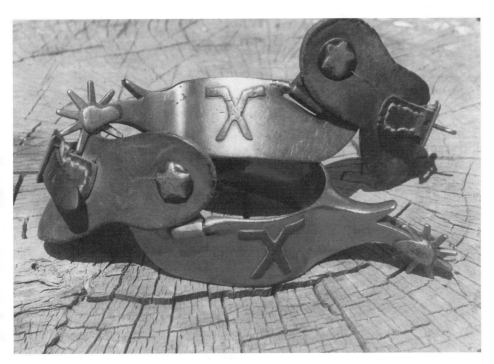

While at Datil, New Mexico, in 1948, Blanchard made a pair of two-piece stainless steel spurs for Joe Pankey. They were unmarked. Joe lost one of the pair, and Ed later made a replacement spur to match. It is marked E. F. BLANCHARD YUCCA ARIZ. *The spurs have the Pankey Flying X brand on the heel band and a star on the outside buttons.* Courtesy Rueben Pankey

This two-piece stainless steel spur is marked E.F. BLANCHARD DATIL N.M. *inside the heel band. It has a chap guard and contoured button straps. The two and three-eighths inch shank has a brass overlay at its base. The shank's tip widens at the end and a brass overlay covers the rowel pin.*
A brass star is on the outside button, and brass initials E R embellish the outside heel band. Courtesy Sue Nowell. Photo by Mel Gnatkowski

Blanchard made this pair of steel spurs with chap guards in 1950 or 1951. He used Mexican coins on the buttons. They are full-mounted with three vertical bars on the inside of the heel bands and Mary Ann Tinguely Kelly's brand, T Bar Lazy T, on the outside bands. The shanks have silver rowel pin covers and a silver bar at the base on the outside. Courtesy Tom Kelly. Photo © Hoss Fosso, 1999

This brass-mounted pair of stainless steel spurs are marked E.F. BLANCHARD DATIL N.M. *inside the heel bands. They have a short shank and the buttons are set unusually far back from the ends of the heel bands.* Courtesy Sue Nowell. Photo by Mel Gnatkowski

This spur is one of a pair of two-piece stainless steel spurs stamped E.F. BLANCHARD MONTICELLO N.M. *inside the heel bands. They are unmounted except for a star on the outside buttons. They are unusual and not a typical Blanchard style. They were probably special-ordered by a customer who wanted the square heel bands and straight buttons.* Courtesy Marty Greenwood. Photo by Mel Gnatkowski

This pair of steel spurs belonged to Bob Cook. Blanchard made them in 1953 when he worked on a ranch northwest of Hyde Park, Arizona. They are stamped E. F. BLANCHARD SELIGMAN ARIZ. *They have the old-style mounting, quarter moons and stars, that were favorites of both Blanchard and Hugh Pankey.* Courtesy Bill Cook

Steel spurs with chap guards made by Blanchard in 1954. They are full-mounted with the old J. P. Kelly brand, the Double Half Circle, on one side of the heel bands and Mary Ann Tinguely Kelly's brand, the T Bar Lazy T, on the opposite bands. Silver covers the rowel pins on both sides of the shanks. Courtesy Tom Kelly. Photo © Hoss Fosso, 1999

Blanchard made this style No. 6 goose-neck spur for Bill Cook in 1975. It is unmounted, stainless steel, and marked E. F. BLANCHARD YUCCA CALIF. Courtesy Bill Cook

This pair of stainless steel spurs made for Mike Kelly at Yucca, Arizona, are some of the last that Ed made before his health failed and he closed his shop. Courtesy Tom Kelly. Photo © Hoss Fosso, 1999

CHAPTER 5

Cowboy Ways

Ed Blanchard worked at various ranches during the early 1930s, but he would go back to the Cooks every so often. One time, Ed and the Cooks were gathering cattle up in the San Mateo Mountains. They had their camp set up at a corral near San Mateo Peak. One morning they were riding near camp when they spotted a wild cow. They roped her and dragged her into camp, where they tied her to a tree. When they got up the next morning, one of the boys handed Ed a cup. "Ed, you go milk that cow, and we'll have cream for our coffee."

This made Ed mad, so he said he'd just pull the damned thing out of the way and tie her somewhere else. That led to a wreck! Ed's horse, Cherry, was bad about rearing up and falling over backward. Ed stepped up on Cherry and rode over to where the cow was tied. He reached down and untied the rope from the tree and took a turn around his saddle horn and started to ride off. Well, of course, Cherry reared up and fell over backward. Off ran the cow, dragging the rope. The Cook boys chased her down and caught her again. This time they tied her farther away from the camp. No one needed milk for his coffee after all.

When Ed made coffee at any outfit's camp, no one could drink it but him. He always got up about 4:00 in the morning. Since he was the first one up, he'd make the coffee. He put a half pound of coffee in a half gallon of water, and he boiled it all day long. Next morning, he poured the other half pound in it. It was so stout that no one could drink it. After he did that a time or two, one of the cowboys would get up at 3:30 ahead of Ed and make the coffee before he could.

They finally cured that problem. Everyone Ed worked for bought him his own pot.

"You drink your coffee," the boys told him, "and we'll drink ours." Ed called them a bunch of sissies.

Needless to say, Ed had his own way of doing things—the old-time way—and it was always the hard way, but many of those old-timers were like that. My dad was. Part of it was that he was hard-headed.

I was home on furlough one time back in 1944. Pop and I were up on Baldy one day, and we caught a horse. My dad put a packsaddle on him and was going to lead him home. We had to come down into Dead Cow Gulch, and it was steep. Pop had put the horn loop of his rope over his saddle horn. We had just dropped off the hill when I noticed it.

"Hey, you'd better take the loop off of your horn," I called to him.

He just ignored me. We got about halfway down the side of the canyon when that packhorse threw a fit. Pop was a little deaf, and he didn't realize what was happening until I hollered at him. The horse had started around him and went below him. Pop was turning his horse around when the packhorse hit the end of the rope and both horses were jerked off-balance. The whole works rolled end over end downhill for three hundred feet.

When they came to a stop, Pop just sat there.

"Didn't you hear me holler at you?" I asked.

"Aw, hell!" he said. "You're always hollering about something!"

He just didn't pay any attention.

Ed was just like that. Tell him not to do something, and that was just what he did.

Every summer Ed liked to work for the Forest Service, because he could do what he wanted. Usually he worked as a fire guard or he had a trail job. It didn't make any difference if he had a thousand

Frank Kelly in Dead Cow Gulch on a more peaceful day than when he had the wreck with the pack horse. Courtesy Tom Kelly

dollars' worth of cattle gathered; when the Forest Service wrote him a letter, he dropped what he was doing and let the cows go to hell. He was off to his Forest Service job.

Ed and Bob Cook were working trail in the San Mateo Mountains one summer in the early 1930s. Ed had taken Bob with him and

[91]

gotten him a job, too. They stayed up on the mountain. Ed was exceptionally clean. He was a pretty good cook and a real clean cook. Everything had to be perfect. He wouldn't even eat with you if he thought your dishes were dirty. He believed in taking a bath every so often, too. Bob said that every Saturday morning, Ed would get him up early and get him on his horse to ride down to the creek for a bath. It was colder than heck up there on top of the mountain, but Ed shucked his clothes and jumped into this big pool of ice-cold water. He made Bob get his Saturday bath, too, even though it was so cold he damn near froze to death.

In 1934, Tally became sheriff of Socorro County, so he hired Ed to run the ranch, and he left the three kids there to help him. But Ed was the boss. I guess it was a pretty big wreck all the time Ed was there. The kids teased him and set traps for him. Ol' Ed stayed mad most of the time, but he kept the thing going for a couple of years.

Each fall, they drove the Cook cattle to Magdalena, the nearest railroad and shipping pens. The cattle carried the Currycomb brand— $\top$ on the left shoulder and $\dashv$ on the left hip. They always had quite a herd, and it was about a fifteen-day drive. They had a chuck wagon and extra horses with them. They camped each night and herded the cattle if there wasn't a corral nearby. They were on the move early each morning.

They drove up the Alamosa River in a northwesterly direction. This was the ancient route taken for centuries by various Indian tribes to Ojo Caliente, the springs at the head of the canyon. The springs were considered neutral ground by the different tribes—Comanches, Kiowas, Utes, and other Plains Indians as well as the Apaches. Near the sheer walls at the mouth of Cañada Alamosa, the river's canyon, the cowboys drove their herd past the springs that feed the river and by the adobe ruins of the army headquarters of the Ojo Caliente (Warm Springs) Indian Agency. The agency was occupied for only three years. During that time, Geronimo and Victorio and their people were held there. They were then moved to the San Carlos Reservation in Arizona in 1877.

The drive continued northwest past Dusty, finally skirting the north end of the San Mateo Mountains, where it entered the stock driveway and circled back eastward to Magdalena.

New Mexico cowboys bring a herd of Longhorn steers into the shipping pens at Magdalena between 1886 and 1890. Courtesy J. E. Smith collection, Socorro, New Mexico

The stock driveway gave cowmen of western New Mexico and eastern Arizona access from the west to the Magdalena shipping pens. It was established by the authority of the secretary of the interior after the ranchers asked that land along their cattle trail be exempt from settlement following the Homestead Act of 1916. The seventy-one thousand acres made a strip of land one-quarter mile to five miles wide. It was fenced and had forage for the herds. Wells supplied water every ten miles. Cowmen used this driveway until about 1960, when trucks replaced the railroad as the means of transporting cattle to market.

One year when Ed was trail boss of the Currycomb cattle on their trip to Magdalena, they reached the Tucker Ranch headquarters about fifteen miles or so from the Currycomb. It was late afternoon, so they put the cattle in Tucker's corral for the night and set up camp nearby. As a joke, about 3:30 in the morning, Frank Tucker turned a sow loose in the corral with the cattle. The cows had never seen a pig, and they stampeded. They tore down the side of the corral and disappeared down the draw in the dark. It was pandemonium as the cowboys tried to get their horses saddled to take after the cattle. The cattle ran until they hit a water gap in a fence line. That slowed most of them down, but they knocked the rocks off of the bottom of the wire, and some of them pushed under the fence. Ed didn't slow down. He tore through the fence in the dark and ripped his shirt off on the barbed wire.

They finally got all the cattle stopped and gathered and went on toward Magdalena with them. The next night, they had to herd them because there was no corral. Ed kept the night horses up and turned the rest of the horses loose. The next morning when Ed went to gather the horses, they were scattered all over the country. They finally got them gathered and headed toward camp. Ed rode on ahead into camp and took two long ropes. He tied one to the wagon and one to a tree, and he told seventeen-year-old Billy Cook to hold those two ropes.

"I'm bringing the horses into this rope corral, so you hang on," he said. "We don't want to lose them again."

Billy held the ropes that formed the V-shaped corral, and Ed, swinging a big loop, brought the horses in at a dead run. After the horses hit that rope, Billy's arms were probably twice as long as before, but they got the horses corralled.

Several days later, Ed and his crew drove into Magdalena after dark and put the herd in the stock pens. Ed set up camp right next to the corral fence. The pens were full of cattle, and they bawled and milled all night. Manure and dust settled over the camp. No one got much sleep that night, and the next morning, the cowboys were unhappy. So Ed moved camp about three-quarters of a mile out on top of a hill east of Magdalena. Then they had all that way to ride to the pens to work their cattle. That's the way he did everything—it was always the hard way.

By this time, 1934, Ed had begun to make spurs. All during this drive, he had griped, "I don't know what I'm doing with this sickening outfit! I could have stayed home and made two pair of spurs." All Ed could think about was making spurs. But more about spurs later.

Jake Potter was a cowboy who hung around the Kelly outfit. Jake could really braid leather, and he made good quirts, but you had to watch him. When he ran short of leather to braid, he'd cut the strings off of your saddle. He and Ed became good friends. Jake was one heck of a cowboy. He would stay out on a ranch somewhere for six months to a year, and he was a hard worker. But he had one little problem. Once he was paid, he went to town and got drunk and stayed drunk until every penny was gone. He'd buy a new hat, Levi's, and a coat and head straight for the bar to play poker and get drunk. When my brother Jim and I were kids, if we could catch him before he got too drunk and lost all his money, he'd buy us cap pistols.

About 1931 or 1932, Ed and Jake became partners in a ranch northwest of Magdalena near the end of the Bear Mountains out toward the Alamo Indian Reservation. Ed knew he couldn't have Jake too close to town. The ranch had twenty sections and ran about one hundred cows in those days. Ed and Jake stocked it with other people's cattle, but they also had a little herd of their own for a while. They didn't keep them there continuously, because they were always going off to work someplace else. Ed also made spurs there at his ranch.

The Kellys put a bunch of cattle over there at first, but the boys didn't stay around and take care of them. The Kellys went back and gathered their cattle and drove them back down to the Flat. Finally Ed and Jake didn't have any cattle there, but they stayed there. Eventually Ed bought ol' Jakie out. I guess he got tired of Jake's trips to town.

When Lilly Blanchard left Water Canyon, her sister, who was my grandmother, bought her cow herd and brand, the Rafter R. When Granny Kelly died in 1932, the Kelly boys took two hundred head of her Rafter R cattle to Ed. I don't know if he bought them or she left them to him, but the Rafter R brand became Ed Blanchard's. Ed kept them until he sold out to Guy Spears some years later. Spears bought the cattle and the brand. Ed's brand had previously been a Double D ⅅ—a small D inside a larger D. It was a horror to brand, since it blotted easily.

The headquarters of Ed and Jake's ranch had a rock house near a big pile of boulders. It was a one-room shack that some previous owner had built, and it sat back in a canyon near a little spring of water. The biggest things around there were the rattlesnakes. Five- to six-foot-long rattlesnakes were everywhere. Ed and Jake were always killing snakes.

The rock walls of this old house had holes that the wind blew through and the varmints crawled in. Ed's bunk was on one wall, and Jake's was across the room. One morning about daylight, Ed woke Jake up. Jake stirred and asked him what he wanted. Ed was whispering, and he had his head under his tarp. Jake told him to speak up—he couldn't hear him.

"There's a rattlesnake in the springs of my bed! Every time I move, it rattles. I'm afraid to get out of bed."

"Well, what do you want me to do about it?" Jake just rolled over and went back to sleep.

Ed was all tucked in so the snake couldn't get to him. When he saw that Jake wasn't going to give him any relief, he finally got up the nerve to get out of bed. He got a stick and poked the snake out so he could kill it. Ed stayed mad at Jake all day.

During the 1930s while Ed had his ranch, Tex Austin produced the annual rodeo in Magdalena. One year, Ed rode into town on his horse, Pard, and hired on as pick-up man to take the riders off of their broncs after they finished their rides. Pard was one of Ed's "good" horses that would buck, rear up, and run off.

After the first performance was over, one of the bronc riders headed for a local bar. A guy at the bar asked, "What kind of broncs do they have this year?"

"Oh, hell, the broncs aren't too bad," the cowboy answered. "They're pretty easy to ride. But watch out for that pick-up man—he'll get you killed!"

Ed was rough, and that horse would either buck or run off every time he'd try to pick a cowboy up. Pard would head across the arena with Ed hollering, "Whoa, you s.o.b.! Whoa!" The bronc rider would be lying back on the ground where Ed had dumped him. The contestants were soon more leery of Ed than they were of the broncs.

Tom Mix came to these Tex Austin Ranch Rodeos at Magdalena. Pop knew him. He said he was one hell of a cowboy. Mix knew a lot of these rodeo contestants, because many of them went to Hollywood during the off-season and worked as extras in the movies. Claude Humphreys was one of those boys. He was a cowboy who wandered in and out of these parts during the 1930s and 1940s. Ol' Hump was a great bronc rider. He often competed at Magdalena. He had a pair of Ed's spurs. In fact, they are the only gal-leg spurs I've ever seen that Blanchard made. They are unmarked and they have HUMP overlaid in silver on the outside heel bands.

Hump was born in the Grants area. We knew him up at Red Lake, north of Magdalena. He managed the cattle for either the Acoma or Laguna Reservation. He married a Navajo woman and in later years had a trading post.

In 1934, while Uncle Tally was Socorro County sheriff, he arrested a man for stealing cattle. It was a big cow-theft case here in Socorro County. It was said that this man was a known cow thief. He supposedly stole a bunch of cattle on the Rio Grande below San Antonio and took them up to his place near Ed and Jake's. He was arrested for burning the brands on these cattle. During the trial, Uncle Tally and some of the court went out to the man's ranch and got one of his cows. They brought it into Socorro and killed it. They skinned it and had all the hide experts testify whether or not the brand had been changed. These "experts" included my dad and Uncle Jim and two or three of the best cow thieves in the county. My father said the brand had never been altered. The cow belonged to the accused man.

The courtroom was full of all the local cattlemen. Ed leaned over and said to Uncle Tally, "Well, by G__, that one there might not have been burned, but the brand on the one Jake and I killed last winter had damned sure been changed! I know 'cause we skinned her out!"

Uncle Tally was trying to shut Ed up, but Ed just kept telling this big ol' honest story.

Someone in the crowd spoke up. "Ed Blanchard—you better watch out. You better not be killing someone else's cows!"

"Well, hell, she came in to water," Ed said. "She was big and fat, and Jake and I were hungry, so we just killed her. And by damn, her brand was burned!"

One year Ed worked for Badger & Bruner, and he and two other cowboys were taking a herd of horses from Magdalena to the Diamond Bar down on the Gila River. When they left Magdalena the first morning, Ed had saddled a little, crazy horse that had never been ridden much.

"Don't ride that horse to drive those horses," Bo Hobbs told Ed. "The damned thing runs off, and you can't stop him."

That was all Ed needed to be more determined to ride that particular horse, and he got on him.

About fifteen miles out, the horse ran off with Ed and stepped in a badger hole. The horse turned about three flips, and Hobbs sent Ed back to Magdalena with a cracked skull. He lay there in the hospital for ten days. The doctors wanted to send him to Albuquerque, but Ed wouldn't go. He said he'd get fired from his job if he stayed in the hospital. He wanted to go back to the ranch. His skull was split down the middle, but they didn't do anything to it. I guess in time it finally grew back together. It didn't seem to hurt him any. He was just as bull-headed as ever.

Ed was such a wild cowboy he was dangerous to be around. Like the time Joe Pankey and Ed were chasing a big two-year-old maverick bull over in the San Mateos. They were going down a steep mountainside into a big canyon. Joe hollered at Ed, "Don't rope him on the hillside. Wait 'til he gets to the bottom of the canyon!"

As usual, the warning did not slow Ed Blanchard down. He tossed his loop and caught the bull by a front foot as they dropped off of the lip of the canyon. Ed's horse went around one side of a tree, and the bull went on the other side. When they both hit the end of the rope, there was a terrible wreck. Ed and his horse finally got up, but it broke the bull's leg. They had to shoot him. Joe was sure mad at Ed, because he didn't wait like he told him to. It cost Joe a bull.

When Ed was down at the Currycomb in the early 1930s, everyone was entitled to homestead 640 acres of land. Uncle Tally and Aunt Mable talked him into homesteading a section of land down the creek on their boundary fence. There was a section of government land up on the hill that would go with it as a lease.

Ed filed the proper papers and built a little shack on the place to prove it up. He paid the filing fee and got the deed. He hadn't had it long when he went to Uncle Tally and offered to sell it for fifty dollars.

"Well, I'll buy it if you will wait until fall," Tally said. "I don't have the money right now, but I'll pay you then."

But Ed didn't wait. He sold the land to one of their neighbors who was one of the biggest enemies the Cooks had. Ed wasn't welcome around the Currycomb for quite a while after that.

Ed's brother Charlie was about eight years older than Ed. Charlie never moved fast, and he never had any real good job, but he always tried and he worked hard. He worked as a carpenter and a carpenter's helper around the country. Every so often Charlie would show up at our house, and he'd be out of a job. I don't remember how he got there. He didn't have a car. Ed must have brought him and dropped him off.

Charlie was even more peculiar than Ed. I guess you have to understand these ol' guys. Those fellows born before 1900 were entirely different from what you see now. They did what they thought they had to do. Most of them were fairly honest in their dealings unless you made enemies of them. Of course, they had their own ways of doing things, and you couldn't change their ways. In my generation, we thought they did everything ass-backward and were so old-fashioned they'd never get anything done. They got a lot done during their lives, but they did it their own way. And they weren't too much on taking orders.

Anyway, Charlie showed up in Water Canyon without a job, so my dad got him a job raking the trails up on Mount Baldy for the Forest Service. Charlie moved about half as fast as most men, and he got tired of the trails pretty fast.

I was about fourteen years old, and one evening my dad unsaddled his horse and came to find me. "You're going to have to go take Charlie's place up on Baldy for about a week," he told me. "Charlie says he's got a bad back."

So we went to Baldy on Monday morning. There was ol' Charlie, lying in bed. He had a rope tied on the rafter to pull himself up and down. He was groaning and dying with his back. I wondered if he had a bad back or not or if he was just tired of raking trails. He told me if I'd do his work for him for a week, he'd pay me.

In those days, they paid sixty to eighty cents an hour, and he worked eight hours a day. I worked for Charlie a week, and he paid me twenty-five cents an hour and kept the difference. But this was the way those old guys were, and you just had to expect it.

It rained and Charlie and my dad were laid off, so they came back home. Charlie didn't want to leave our house because it was a good place to putter around, and he got plenty to eat. My mother soon had him fixing little things around the house.

The folks had to go to town one day, and Mother asked Charlie, "Will you solder my washtubs while we're gone? They've got holes in the bottoms." Ol' Charlie was a pretty good handyman and could fix anything.

We lived in a two-story log house that my dad had built in 1930. My brother and I were upstairs, snooping around through our dresser drawers, and we found three or four giant firecrackers that they made in those days. They were about four inches long, and if you put one of those firecrackers under a tin can, it would blow the can way up in the air.

We looked out the window, and there was ol' Charlie in the yard, squatted down soldering away on a washtub with a soldering iron. We thought it would be a good laugh to open the window and drop a firecracker out beside him. We lit one and dropped it down there. The damned thing hit the ground and bounced right under Charlie's rear end. When that firecracker blew, Charlie launched up and out six feet or more. He and the tub made about three rolls before he crawled out from under it.

He looked all around and shook his head. It must have almost blown his eardrums out. He was trying to get his marbles back together, and we were dying laughing. Charlie looked up and saw us. He picked up his soldering iron and headed around the house to the back door. We waited until we heard him coming up the stairs, and then we went out the window and climbed down the logs at the corner of the house as fast as we could. We lit out and didn't go back to the house until after the folks came home.

Poor ol' Charlie was still rubbing his ears and shaking his head that evening. The next day, he was in a pretty good humor, so I guess we were forgiven. He stayed around for another month, and then off he went. We didn't see him again for four or five years.

CHAPTER 6

The Forge and the Anvil

Ed was living at the Currycomb when he went to Rueben Pankey's ranch about 1931. The Pankey headquarters was south of Socorro down by Nogal, fifteen or twenty miles from the Currycomb.

Rueben Pankey was an old-time Texas cowman. He had been up the trail to Dodge City and to Hugo, Colorado, and also to the Musselshell River in Montana. He had worked on ranches throughout Texas, New Mexico, and Mexico. In 1898, he started his own ranch south of Hillsboro, New Mexico, and in 1920 sold it for $187,000. He moved to Hot Springs and soon purchased several ranches in the area, including the Morine Ranch.

The Pankeys had four sons—Joe, Hugh, Lee, and Bill. Joe and Lee both worked in Florida for a short time, but they returned to the family ranch in Sierra County. Joe, the oldest, bought the Flying X Ranch from his father in 1920 and operated 110 sections in rugged Sierra County between Rueben's ranch and the Currycomb.

*The barns and pens on the east side of the highway that runs south from
Socorro through the old Rueben Pankey ranch headquarters near Nogal.
It was here at headquarters that Hugh Pankey taught Blanchard
the art of spur making.* Photo by Jane Pattie

Hugh Pankey was quite a blacksmith. He worked for many of the
local mines for several years, and he also learned to make spurs. He
was a good spur maker, but that was not his trade. He was a cowboy,
but once in a while he made a pair of spurs for one of the other
cowboys. He lived back up a canyon about five miles from the Pankey
headquarters.

Hugh was making spurs in the 1920s, and he taught Ed Blanchard
how to make spurs during the early 1930s. Ed copied Hugh's spurs
in the beginning, except he normally set the buttons at more of an
angle than Hugh did. He also usually cut out the bands behind the
button straps so the buttons lay flat—but not always at first. Bill Benton
cowboyed with Ed at the C Bar N Ranch when Ed was first making
spurs, and Benton said that he and Ed came up with the off-set button to make his spurs fit better. In Ed's one-piece plain steel spurs,
the button hangers were bradded onto the heel bands. Sometimes

the hangers were straight, but very soon they were always angled unless the customer requested otherwise.

Hugh Pankey made a pair of spurs in 1942 for Felix Martinez, and I thought Blanchard had made them. I guess by that time, Hugh copied Ed. Hugh made spurs for twenty or thirty years, but he never made a large number, and to my knowledge, he never sold any. He made them for friends. Anyway, in the beginning Ed stayed at the Pankeys' for a while and practiced spur making with Hugh's advice.

When Ed returned to the Currycomb sometime during 1932, he tried making a pair of spurs on his own. Billy Cook recalls that the first pair Ed made was rather crude-looking. They had a lot of hammer marks on them, and they'd eat the heels out of your boots because he didn't file them off on the inside. But he kept practicing, and he quickly improved. He made each one of the Cook boys a pair with the 6K Bar 6K̲ brand on the heel band. He also made Tally Cook a pair with the Currycomb brand—T̅ ⊣—and a pair with a Heart Bar ♡ brand for Mable. These spurs were one-piece and unmarked but typical of Blanchard's early spurs. A thief stole them out of the Cooks' house in Kingman years later after they moved to Arizona.

The Rueben Pankey collection of spurs made by Hugh Pankey and Ed Blanchard. Courtesy Rueben Pankey

When Ed began making spurs in the early 1930s, a blacksmith in Magdalena named Willenstein had a stack of Model T axles, and Ed bought them. They were made of tempered steel. For several years, he made his spurs out of the axles, and they were real good spurs. Those axles lasted a long time. Spur making was hard work. Ed made me a pair of kid's spurs in 1932 or 1933. They are small, and they have a lot of mounting and my initials, TK, on the heel bands. By the time he made these spurs, he had been at it long enough to be a good craftsman.

I'll never forget the day Ed gave me those spurs. The kids from Water Canyon went to school in Magdalena, and we rode the bus back and forth. We came home one afternoon and got off the bus down at the Flat. Ed was waiting at the gate where Lucy and J. B. Kelly and I got off the bus, and he handed me those spurs. They were the shiniest, prettiest things I had ever seen. I still have them.

Back in those days, spurs were really handmade. Ed cut a length of axle and split it with a chisel and a hacksaw. He heated it. Then he hammered it out flat and beat it around a piece of wagon axle to shape the band. He had an old Blücher boot he kept in his shop, and he'd beat those spurs until they exactly fit that boot heel. He shaped the shank however he wanted it. During these early years, Ed had few tools, and what he did have, he made himself.

After he had made a few pairs, he got pretty good at it. I doubt that he made more than twenty pairs before 1935, and he gave those to his friends and relatives. Toward the end of the 1930s, he made some really pretty spurs. In fact, his best spurs were made between 1933 and about 1945. He put a lot of work into them, and they were of good steel and had a lot of mounting.

I ordered a pair of spurs from Ed for my dad in 1944. They were one-piece. I also ordered a pair for my brother in 1946, and Ed was still making one-piece spurs. None of these early spurs were marked. He had no way of stamping his name in them. They were all made out of good steel—probably car axles. He'd look in all the trash pits to find a piece of good steel.

In the early days, Ed mounted a lot of his spurs, and he often used copper as well as silver. He solicited help from my brother and me when we were little kids. "There are some old copper double boilers around here in the canyon," he'd say. "I'll give you a dollar for each one you can find."

We really got busy. We finally found one half-buried up the creek and dug it up and got our dollar. Ed used that for his copper mountings. For silver mountings, he first used knives or forks or any silver-colored metal. Of course, he couldn't use silver plate, because when he heated it, the silver veneer would melt off. But he used sterling silver dishes. It wasn't safe to have a sterling silver sugar bowl around. It would probably wind up as spur mounts.

The best silver the local spur makers used was Harvey House silverware. Fred Harvey offered good food to train travelers at his restaurants along the Atchison, Topeka & Santa Fe Railway. He opened his first lunchroom in Kansas in 1878, and he soon had exclusive rights to serve food at AT&SF stations west of the Mississippi River. Harvey Houses were scattered up and down the line and through New Mexico at Las Vegas, Albuquerque, San Marcial, and so on. The Santa Fe had a roundhouse at San Marcial, south of Socorro. The railroad workers from the roundhouse as well as train travelers ate at the Harvey House. Many a local rancher ate there, too, when in the area, and he could easily slip a spoon or two in his pocket when he left. The metal was tough and possibly German silver. A fork or spoon handle was thick and heavy and easy to make into silver mounting for spurs. So Harvey House restaurants helped embellish a lot of spurs.

Ed wasn't the only one who used Harvey House silver. When I was about ten years old, my dad and I stayed at a neighbor's ranch one night. They had all kinds of Harvey House silverware. I later asked my dad about it, and he said the rancher's wife had a rule. Every time her husband went down to the Harvey House at San Marcial, he had to bring back a piece of silver, so that's how she got her silverware for the house. The cowboys would also slip out with a knife or fork or spoon and bring them to her.

Back in those days, the ranchers used copper floats to cut the water off in the water troughs. Ed used anything he could get that was made of copper for mountings, and those floats were a good source. He made his brass mountings from old well cylinders that were worn out and had been discarded. He always picked them up when he found them. If he didn't have any silver spoons or forks, he used a dime or a fifty-cent piece and hammered it out real thin. I know that when he first started selling spurs, he used dimes on the buttons. On some of those early spurs, you can still see the pictures on the dimes. He hammered them out to just the size of the buttons, which were made from carriage bolts. When he learned it was illegal to deface United States money, he began using Mexican coins for his mountings.

I had Ed make me a pair of stainless steel spurs in 1947. He hadn't made many stainless steel spurs before that. He had learned to weld somewhere, and from then on many of his spurs were two-piece, with the shanks welded onto the heel bands. But he still made a good spur out of fairly heavy metal. When he started making stainless steel spurs about 1946 or 1947, he began stamping his name in them and also SS, for stainless steel.

The first spurs that had Ed's name in them were probably made at Datil. He worked for Ranger Arthur Gibson of the Forest Service as a fire guard and stayed at the old Baldwin Ranger Station for three or four months every summer. He had a horse and rode up on Sugar Loaf Mountain and around watching for fires, but in the evenings and early in the mornings, he made spurs. Ed's work with the Forest Service was usually over in July, but Gib let him stay on the rest of the summer and make spurs. The place had a garage, and Ed had his forge and anvil set up in there. All the spurs stamped DATIL N.M. were made in that garage.

During the winters, Ed went back to Monticello and stayed with the Cooks. He marked those spurs MONTICELLO N.M. A collector can pretty well tell the years his spurs were made by the way they are marked. I know he was in Datil from 1940 through 1948 in the summers, and he was making spurs.

That last summer, 1948, we had cattle west of Datil near Swingle Canyon, right across the road from the ranger station. The Forest Service had made us move our cattle off of Baldy to "rest" the land, and Pop had leased this land at Datil. We leased our horse pasture from Mrs. Nourse for five dollars a month, and we stayed in a tent we set up in a grove of pine trees. Ed said he wanted to ride with us again—it had been so many years since he had. So he arrived in camp real early one morning to help gather cattle. He had had his breakfast, and we had, too. We finished washing the dishes and put them away in an old metal footlocker.

We saddled our horses and headed out to gather cattle. We worked all morning. Pop and Ed were getting along good, talking about things that had happened fifty years before. About three o'clock, we went back to camp to cook dinner. My dad began mixing up the dinner, and Ed rolled up his shirt sleeves. "I guess I'll just wash them dishes up a little. They probably got dirty settin' there today," Ed said.

That flew all over my dad. "Damn you, Ed Blanchard! Keep your hands out of the dishes or go home! We washed them this morning and they're clean!" Ed was extra clean with his cooking, and he hated flies. But he backed off from rewashing the dishes that day. He sat down and ate steak and potatoes and seemed to enjoy it even if he wasn't sure the dishes were clean.

When Ed had arrived in camp that morning, he got to telling us about this wonderful horse he had had. He had killed him by accident about two weeks before. He was a black, streak-faced horse that Uncle Jim had given him. I remembered him. He was a real good-looking horse but meaner than holy heck. He was about eight years old. He bucked every time Ed got on him and did his best to throw him. He'd kick you or paw you, but that was the best horse Ed ever had, to hear him tell it. He went over all the horse's good points.

He told my dad, "I killed the best G__-damned horse I ever had!" Ed cussed in those days. He said he was driving up the highway between Socorro and Magdalena and his pickup got to weaving. The old horse was in the back in a set of racks. Pretty soon, the truck shot off the road, made some big wobbles, and almost turned over. That horse fell out of those racks onto the ground, and the fall killed him.

Big tears started running down Ed's cheeks.

Pop just looked at him. "It's too bad that damned horse didn't kill you before you killed him! Then everything would have been all right!"

That was the last we heard of Ed's good black horse.

During the time we had cattle at Datil in 1948, Ed was supposed to be building a pair of plain steel spurs for me. One night after I got through riding, I went down to the ranger station. It was just about dark, but Ed was still in the garage, where he had his forge and anvil. He could hardly see, but he was pounding away, shaping a spur. I tried to talk to him, but he was so busy pounding, he would hardly talk. It finally got so dark he couldn't see.

"Let's go in the house, and I'll make a pot of coffee," he said. I already knew about his coffee. I didn't figure I wanted any, but I said I'd come in and visit.

We went inside and it was dark—there was no electricity. Ed had a big kitchen table about six feet long and three or four feet wide. He had an oilcloth over the top of it, and there was a Coleman lantern sitting in the middle of the table.

"I sure hate it, but I guess we're going to have to light that damn lantern," he said.

"You want me to light it for you?" I asked.

"Oh, hell, no. I've been lighting it forever. It's just hard to get the sickening thing to burn," he said.

He pumped the lantern up real big and got a match in his hand. He turned the lamp up full blast and threw the match on the table. Woof! Flames shot up everywhere, and the ol' lantern started burning.

"See what I mean?" he said. "It sure is hard to light one of them things."

"Ed, do you light that lantern like that every night?" I asked.

"Yeah. That's the only way you can make it burn."

I wondered if I would ever get my spurs.

When Ed finished his summer work in Datil each year, he'd go back to the Currycomb. The spurs stamped MONTICELLO could have been made anytime from 1946 to 1949, because he made spurs there in the winter during those years. Many of his unstamped spurs were also made earlier at the Currycomb Ranch.

By 1948, the Forest Service was no blessing to ranchers. At that time, the Cooks had two ranches—one near Lamy and the Currycomb. The Currycomb was seventy-five sections, or forty-eight thousand acres. Some of that was grazing rights on Forest Service land. The Cooks ran 800 to 1,000 head of cattle, but the Forest Service kept cutting back on the number of cattle they could run until they were allowed only 150 head. They could not make it with so few cattle. The Forest Service did that to all the ranchers. The Cooks finally sold out and left New Mexico in 1949 to get away from the federal government's grazing rules. They went to Arizona.

After the Cooks sold the ranch, Ed stayed there for a year and worked for the new owner. About all he did was to make spurs. I never thought his two-piece welded spurs were as good as the one-piece spurs he made earlier. He didn't put as much mounting on them, because he was busy with more orders. It wasn't yet a continuous job for him, but he'd get four or five orders and make his spurs at night. Working that way, it took him about a week to make a pair. By 1948, if he worked on spurs steadily, he could make a pair in two days. These were the welded, two-piece spurs, filed and polished and mounted.

Ed got ten dollars for a pair of spurs in 1940. We tried to get him to charge more for his spurs. He wouldn't do it at the time. Cowboys were earning thirty dollars a month, and Ed figured if he could make a pair a week, he was more than doubling his income.

In 1944, he did go up in price to fifteen dollars, and about 1948 he sold his spurs for twenty dollars. Then he went to thirty dollars and to forty dollars. When he had a stroke and quit making spurs in the 1970s, he was charging fifty dollars a pair. That's the most he ever got. It was a poor occupation, but if he worked fourteen to sixteen hours a day, he made pretty good money.

Beginning in the 1930s, Ed had a pickup truck and he hauled his camp gear and his bedroll and equipment from ranch to ranch while he was still cowboying. He also had his anvil and forge and pieces of steel and copper and an old brass cylinder. When he had time at night and if the ranch had a shop where he could set up, he'd make spurs. Sometimes he didn't take his tools with him, but if a ranch had a pretty good blacksmith shop, Ed liked to work there. Spur making was a disease to him.

You've heard of old-timers who would prospect night and day, hunting for a rich strike. They were said to have "gold fever." That's the way Ed was with spurs. If he was working at something else, he'd say, "I could have made two pair of spurs while I was doing this." He was always saying that the work he had to do was keeping him from making spurs.

It is my opinion that the very first spurs he made are the ones he gave me when I was small. He also gave several pairs away to his friends. Probably another of those first spurs he made he gave to George Latham, one of the Pankeys' cowboys. They're different from the ones he made a little later, and my spurs are different from those made in the 1930s. I've seen four pairs of his spurs made before 1935. They're all well made, but they have a few hammer marks on them where he beat them on the anvil. But he put good mountings on them. Ed's only equipment was a forge, a hammer, and an anvil.

In those days, he mounted most of his spurs. Some are mounted with a heart, diamond, club, or spade on one side of the heel band and a name or initials or brand on the other side. Those spurs were probably made between 1933 and 1940. He did a lot of mounting during those years. On the inside heel band, he often put three bars—one of copper, one of brass, and one of silver. Sometimes they were straight up and down, and sometimes they were slanted. He might use copper and brass on the inside mounting and silver on the outside. The mounting probably depended on the material he had on hand.

He also decorated the spur shanks. He often put a large copper or brass plate on the shank where it butts into the heel band, and he always put a piece of silver over the rowel pin. He mounted some of his earlier spurs with silver on one button and copper or brass on the other button. Sometimes he left the outside button plain, but more often than not, he overlaid it with a silver, brass, or copper five-point star. He did that for many years. But he never put mounting on the inside band unless the customer ordered it that way.

Ed Blanchard made a lot of spurs to order. Sometimes a cowboy had lost one spur and needed it replaced. He would give Ed his spur, and Ed would make one to match. So some of the spurs he made do not look like Blanchard spurs because they are copies of someone else's style. It would be hard to decide if Ed made those spurs or not unless he put his name in them, and I doubt that he would have.

The stainless steel spurs he made for me in 1947 were stamped E.F.B. DATIL, N.M. Those spurs were too big for me, so I sold them in 1948 to a man who worked for me, and I had Ed make me another pair out of regular steel. That was the pair he was working on when we had cattle at Datil. He did not stamp those with his name. He just stamped my initials under the button. So he didn't always put his name in them even after he had the tools to do it. Sometimes if he made spurs for a friend, he left his name out of them or stamped them E.B. or E.F.B. and the location where he made them—maybe DATIL N.M. or MONTICELLO N.M. But most of his spurs that are marked have his full name—ED F. BLANCHARD and the location inside of the heel band. He often marked his stainless steel spurs with SS, the plain steel spurs with PS, and the tool steel, TS.

When Ed began making spurs, he didn't make any special styles. His early spurs had sharper rowels than those he made in later years. He made some with goose-neck shanks and some with a curved, turned-down shank. From the beginning, he made some spurs with chap guards and some without. Some spurs had nine-point rowels, and some had smaller rowels with more points, but those first hand-made rowels were pretty sharp.

Ed told me that he changed his style of rowels about 1960, because a lot of these so-called cowboys were mean to their horses. He named three fellows who got dull rowels when they ordered spurs. He didn't want them spurring their horses and tearing up their hides. He said there were some people he wouldn't even make spurs for, because they were too hard on horses.

Unless someone ordered a special mounting, you can usually tell by the mounting about when the spurs were made. Ed's early spurs, beginning in 1932, had a lot of mounting, and it was usually the same. Mounting from that period was often the three bars and the playing card symbols. Sometimes he put a large copper diamond on the heel band or maybe a diamond of brass with a silver heart in the middle of it.

In the early days, he often decorated the heel band with a quarter moon on either side of a five-point star, also a favorite mounting of Hugh Pankey's. Some are mounted that way on the inside and some on the outside. It depended on if the cowboy wanted his brand or initials on them or just single mountings. He did that up until about 1940 and maybe as late as 1943.

From 1941 until 1946, Ed sometimes soldered a flat piece of silver on the outside of the band, and if a cowboy wanted his initials on the spurs, he stippled the background of the plate with a file, leaving the raised initials smooth. He made quite a few pairs like that in the early 1940s. He made spurs of that style at Datil or they could have been made on a ranch somewhere. I know he made that style on the Flat at Jim Kelly's ranch. Those spurs made at Uncle Jim's ranch had no markings on them.

During part of 1948 and 1949, Ed worked at the Currycomb Ranch and made spurs there. When the Cooks sold the place, he helped them gather their cattle and ship them. But he made spurs, too. He stamped all those spurs MONTICELLO, N.M. After the Cooks left, Ed stayed at the ranch about eight months, worked for the new owner, and made spurs at night.

Ed wasn't in Datil after 1948. He had good reason to avoid the area. He had been at Datil all summer in 1948, working for the Forest Service and making spurs in his spare time. He didn't have a thought in his mind except the next pair of spurs he would make, and for sure he had no thoughts of women.

As luck would have it, there was an "old maid" living nearby who had been reared in that part of New Mexico. She wasn't the most beautiful woman in the area nor the handiest to be around nor the sexiest thing to stumble out of the Datil Mountains, but she sure was a native. She was a little odd—strange—honestly, she was crazy as hell! She rode around bareback on an ol' paint horse. She was about forty years old, ten or fifteen years younger than Ed.

One day she wandered down to Ed's and discovered him in his shop, turning the crank on his forge and beating out a spur on the anvil. Soon she was turning the crank for him and visiting with him. She began coming around more often, turning Ed's crank and telling him how the West was won. For sure, Ed never let her in the house. They just stayed out in that old garage, she cranking and Ed pounding away on spurs.

All this friendliness was really getting to Ed. "She shore is makin' me itchy!" he'd say, but he couldn't come up with a way to run her off. I don't know how long this pounding and crank turning went on, but she finally made the fatal mistake.

Ed's birthday was coming up in September, so this bareback-riding woman decided to set a trap for Ed. She sent out a few invitations through the Datil mail to local people inviting them to a surprise birthday party for Ed Blanchard. She explained that the first surprise was to be the party, and the second surprise was that she was going to propose marriage to Ed during the event.

Of course, somebody let the cat out of the bag by showing an invitation to Ed and asking him about it.

Well, ol' Ed disappeared so fast that Ben Lilly's pack of lion dogs couldn't have trailed him up and ever found him. Ed headed back to Water Canyon and the Currycomb and did his own cranking. We tried to kid him a little about this almost fatal wreck, but we got no comment.

My dad said he could just see Ed and this ol' gal riding double bareback up the draw on her paint horse, each with a Blanchard spur on one foot or the other, going on their honeymoon. We thought that was funny, but Ed saw no humor in it at all. That was the end of Ed's work at Datil.

From the later part of 1949 into 1952, he stayed in the Water Canyon area. He had a herd of cattle that the Tuckers pastured for him out at Dusty. Then he leased a little ranch from Ed Burris south of Socorro and moved those cattle down there. He had about fifty head. He put them in the Burris pasture between today's I-25 and the Rio Grande, and he made spurs there at Ed Burris's for two or three years. I used to stop there and visit him. All of those spurs were stamped with his name and SAN ANTONIO, N.M. They were made from 1950 until early 1952. Nothing remains of the Burris place. It was bulldozed when the highway was built.

Ed got the "Cooks disease" again in 1952, and he wanted to go to the Cooks, who were now in Arizona. They had gone to Kingman and bought a big ranch that covered seventy sections in the mountains and a hundred sections on the desert. I assume that Ed sold his cattle. Anyhow, he gathered all of his belongings and went to Arizona. He got as far as Seligman and took a job on a ranch northwest of there near Hyde Park. He made spurs at night in the ranch's shop whenever he could. He wasn't there for long, so there are not many spurs marked SELIGMAN, ARIZ.

Ed made his acetylene for welding with carbide, and it was explosive. One night he left his carbide on, and about 3:00 A.M., it blew the end out of that rancher's garage and shop.

"I just don't think I can use you any longer, Ed," the rancher told him.

"He didn't fire me," Ed later said. "He just told me he couldn't use me any longer."

Ed went to western Arizona in 1953 and bought a twenty-section ranch forty-five miles southeast of Yucca on the Bill Williams River. He paid down on it with money he had saved. Porter Cook bought a house in Kingman and had it moved to the ranch for Ed. Ed pastured some yearlings for a while and made spurs. He sometimes had trouble making his payments, and the Cook boys often made payments on his notes. He finally sold this little ranch for twenty thousand dollars, and after that he was strictly a spur maker, but he was able to repay the Cooks.

He moved up closer to Yucca, and from then on, all his spurs were made on his place near Yucca, Arizona. He lived in a simple frame house at the end of a dirt road. There, in a corrugated iron shop behind his house, he made the most spurs he ever made. He also added some equipment that helped to speed up his operation.

Ed told me while he was at Datil it had taken him two days to make a pair of one-piece spurs. Once he began welding them and got some machinery to help him, he could make a pair in sixteen hours. If he didn't have to do too much mounting, he could turn out a pair a day by himself. He also had a local machine shop stamp his rowels out. He soon had spurs scattered all over the western United States and in a lot of other places, too. He had more orders than he could fill.

After he was in Yucca, his brother Charlie showed up. Charlie had gotten old and he couldn't find work, so he went to Arizona to help Ed. Ed already had a man helping him, but Charlie did part of the polishing and he sawed out mountings for the overlays.

By that time, Ed was making two pairs a day and sometimes he could average three pairs a day if everyone worked. His hours were from daylight to dark. Of course, he never kept anyone hired for long, because he wanted to pay people the minimum wage for eight hours and work them twelve to fourteen hours. Therefore, no one lasted very long.

"I had a real good hired hand," he would say. "He worked for me for six months, and I don't know what happened to him. He got mad and quit." Well, he didn't want to work those long hours, and he couldn't live on what Ed paid him.

I often had someone ask who made my spurs, and I would tell him. The cowboy would write Ed a letter and tell him what he wanted. In a month or two, Ed would get the spurs made and sent to the man, and the customer would send him ten dollars or whatever the price was at the time. Over a period of time, about everyone in this country had a pair of Blanchard spurs, and they began to get out into other states, too. People would see them and ask who made them. Ed soon had a good business. He often had so many orders he would be six months behind in filling them.

The key to Ed's spurs was that they fit your boots. When you ordered spurs, Ed always asked what size boot you wore. If it was size 10, 11, or 12, Ed made a long spur. If you wore a smaller boot, the heel band was shorter. Therefore, the spurs fit properly.

You could put most factory-made spurs on and see daylight between the spur and your boot heel. They weren't made right to fit the heel, so they'd work up. I think that was because many had narrow bands. Those spurs never sat right on your heels or stayed where they were supposed to hang. A lot of people wore spurs with tie-down straps that ran under their insteps, but Ed's spurs didn't need them. They never moved. He told me their secret was in the angle of the swinging buttons and the width of the heel band.

It's hard to compare Ed's spurs to Hugh Pankey's, because I've only seen two pairs of Hugh's spurs. One pair he made in 1922 and one pair was made in 1942. He gave one pair to his brother, and the other he made for George Latham, who cowboyed for the Pankeys for many years. Hugh made more spurs than that, but I don't know who has them.

Pankey set his buttons at a little angle, but he didn't cut the top edge of the band out where the button strap could swing clear in like Ed did. But Hugh Pankey's and Ed Blanchard's early spurs were very similar. The first pair of spurs Ed made were like Hugh's—the front ends of the heel bands were square. Ed rounded them a little but not much; they were pretty square. After a while, he got to rounding them off quite a bit. They looked better and fit better. But the slanted buttons were the key to the fit of Blanchard spurs.

Ed told me that he had tried for two years to patent that button, but he could never get it done. The U.S. Patent Office told him there were so many different spurs and buttons they wouldn't patent a button. He should have hired a patent attorney, and he would probably have gotten it done. Even before he died, there were many copies of his spurs being made. It's hard to tell those spurs from the ones Ed made, but he was the first to set his buttons like that. That was the whole point of his spurs—they stayed on your heels where they were supposed to, and they didn't scar your boots.

In the last years that Ed made spurs, his styles were sleek and simple. They had little embellishment, but they were unique and balanced. One might say they were dynamically correct. That is a term not often used with spurs. Of all the old-time makers, Ed Blanchard would have been the last man expected to make spurs in this modernistic style.

CHAPTER 7

Handmade to Order

While Ed had his twenty-section Arizona ranch, the Cook boys—Porter, Billy, and Bob—helped him with his cattle work. Ed's ranch was close to theirs. Ed was always so busy making spurs, he didn't have time to take care of the cows he had.

One morning, Ed and Charlie came rushing into the Cooks' ranch. "My cattle are out of water," Ed told Billy. "I think my well's dry!" He wanted the Cook boys to go to his ranch and look at his well. They had a jeep with a winch on it, so they gathered up their well tools and followed Ed and Charlie over to the well.

A bunch of thirsty yearlings stood around that old dug well. I don't know how deep it was, but Billy said you could look down in it fifty feet or so and see water. It wasn't dry. They discussed it and decided to send Ed down to have a look. They had a pulley and an old ore bucket, so they hooked the winch onto the bucket, and Ed climbed in. Billy worked the winch and Charlie just stood around watching. Porter directed the operation.

The Tom Kelly collection of spurs made by Blanchard.
Photo © Hoss Fosso, 1999. Courtesy Tom Kelly

Porter motioned to let the bucket down, and it soon was out of sight. Porter kept motioning down, down, down, then stop. Ed hollered to pull him up. Soon Ed appeared. "There's water down there, but I don't think there's enough," he said.

"Is the pipe in the water?" Porter asked.

"I didn't get that far down, but it looked like it might be."

"We'll let you down again and you take a better look!" Porter could get a little ornery, and he was aggravated. Porter was also a big tease. Those Cook boys had about driven Ed crazy when they were kids.

Ed climbed back in the bucket, and Billy let him back down real slow. Porter kept motioning down, down. Charlie had on a little hat with an inch-wide brim—one of those city hats. He wandered over and looked down the well. He threw that hat in the air and got to jumping around and screaming, "Edward! Edward!"—they always called each other Edward and Charles—very formal.

"What in the world is wrong with you?" Porter said.

"Edward's gone," Charlie said as he peered down the well. "He's completely gone! His hat's floating on top of the water!"

Porter had let Billy drop Ed down under the water so he could get a good look this time. Charles was having a screaming fit, so they pulled Ed up. He had had a good bath. He reported that there was fifteen feet of water in the well. After they changed the leathers on the sucker rod, they had plenty of water for the cattle. That's how the Cook boys fixed Ed's well.

Ed drove out to the Cooks' ranch another time for a visit. There was a kid there, and his pickup had quit running. It was quite a way back to town. Ed was going to Kingman, so he told this boy he'd hook onto his pickup and pull him into town where he could get his truck worked on.

Ed had a thirty-foot nylon rope with a horn loop in the end, and he put the loop over the ball of his trailer hitch and tied the other end onto the bumper of the pickup. They each got in their trucks, and Ed took off.

Billy saw the kid later. "Did you get to town all right?" he asked.

"I never had such a wild trip in my life! That old fool drove forty

The Cook brothers are pictured on their Arizona ranch during the early 1950s. Bob Cook is standing on the right, Porter is kneeling in the middle, and Bill Cook is leaning at the left. The cowboy in front of Bill was a helper. Blanchard followed the Cooks to western Arizona in 1953. Courtesy Tom Kelly

miles an hour on that dirt road. The dust was so thick, I couldn't see the road. The only time I could see where I was going was when he'd go around a turn. Then I'd swing way out on the flat before I could get turned back onto the road."

When they got to the edge of Kingman, Ed pulled over and stopped. He walked back to the kid's truck. "Where do you want me to take you?"

"Right here is just fine!" The boy wasn't about to let Ed pull him through town.

Ed drove about like he rode a horse. He just aimed it in the direction he wanted to go. He was stiff from his many wrecks on horseback, and when he was in his pickup, he never turned his head to look beside him or behind him. Those old-timers never looked in the mirror. They said everything was "wrong" in the mirror. I learned that when Ed backed up, I sure better help him, because if there was anything around, he'd run over it. He gunned the motor, let out the clutch, and blew away like he was taking off in a jet plane. He never had any wrecks, so I guess he got around better than we thought he did. Maybe his saving grace was that he didn't drive very fast, but he drove the same speed on a dirt road that he did on the highway, and he didn't slow down for curves.

One year Ed and Charlie headed off across Texas to visit some of their relatives. I doubt that they had ever used a road map—they just navigated by dead reckoning. Of course, they got lost, but they finally found their way back to New Mexico and familiar surroundings. It was quite an adventure. "We shore did see a lot of country!" Charlie stated.

Ed was in Datil when he first began sending spurs to some of the saddle shops and feed stores around the country. I know he sent spurs to Brown's Saddle Shop in Albuquerque back in the late 1940s and early 1950s. After he was in Arizona, he had quite a few orders from feed stores and saddle shops, including Harms Feed Store south of Albuquerque as well as Brown's Saddle Shop. He also sold spurs to Windy Ryon's in Fort Worth, Texas.

One of his major customers was N. Porter Company in Phoenix. Porter's had been in business since 1875, and Ed sent them lots of spurs through the years. They advertised them in their catalogs. The Porter Catalog No. 38, issued in the 1950s, pictures the four spurs that Ed advertised in his original brochure. They are priced at $15 and $15.50 for tool steel and $20 and $20.50 for stainless steel. Porter's sold a lot of Blanchard spurs. He generally sent plain, unmounted spurs to the saddle shops and feed stores.

Porter's eventually had financial troubles, and they owed Ed money on spurs. They wrote him not to send any more because they couldn't pay him, but Ed kept making spurs and sending them anyway. He said Porter's had been around ever since he was born, so he knew they'd pay him when they could. They finally owed him fifteen hundred dollars or so when they entered bankruptcy. Whoever handled the bankruptcy eventually sent Ed a check for what they owed him, just like he expected.

After Ed moved to Yucca in 1959, he began getting more spur orders, and spur making became a full-time job. He still made a few bits to order, but once he really got busy with spur orders, he discontinued the bits. He was always two to six months behind on his orders. If you wrote to him and ordered a pair of spurs, your order went to the bottom of the stack, and he worked down to it. He was very conscientious about making every pair of spurs exactly to order.

While in Yucca, Ed began advertising his spurs by sending out brochures with photos of his four styles of spurs: No. 2, a goose-neck spur; No. 3, a bronc spur; No. 4, a drop shank spur with a chap guard; and No. 5, the Bill Simon Cutting Horse Spur. These were the four styles he made to send to the feed stores and saddle shops that sold them. They had no embellishment and could be ordered in stainless steel or plain steel. Stainless steel spurs cost $3 to $5 more, depending on the style. During the 1960s, his price for the stainless steel spurs was $23.50 and the plain steel was $16.50. Brands or initials or any kind of silver mounting was an additional $5. By 1969, he had gone up $3 on spurs, and silver mounting was $10.

Once he began distributing his brochures, Ed not only marked his spurs E. F. BLANCHARD, YUCCA ARIZ, but he also stamped them in the heel band—PS for plain steel, SS for stainless steel, or TS for tool steel, followed by the style number of the spur as pictured in his brochure.

During the 1970s, Ed's brochure pictured six spurs. He had added two styles—No. 6 and No. 8, with variations in the shanks and in the width and length of the heel bands. He had once again raised his prices. His most expensive style was the stainless steel Bill Simon Cutting Horse Spur priced at $39.50.

By the 1970s, Ed had quit sawing out his rowels by hand and filing them and was having them stamped out at a local machine shop. "They have a machine that will cut a dozen at a time for seventy-five cents a piece," Ed told Jane Pattie in 1973. "That's cheaper and easier than I can make them. My time is worth more than that."

Blanchard liked to make the plain spurs for saddle shops and feed stores throughout the West because he could make them quicker since they weren't special order. He worked on two pairs at a time, and when he finished five or ten pairs he would send them to the stores that ordered them. Since plain spurs took less time, he gave the stores a 20 percent discount on them. It is not unusual to find spurs Ed made that have mounting that was added by other craftsmen, which is easily recognized. They were probably bought as unmounted spurs from a saddle shop and decorated by a local artisan. Bill Swope of Cherokee, Texas, has such a pair of Blanchard spurs with mounting that appears to be the work of Adolph Bayers of Truscott, Texas.

After Ed opened his shop in Yucca, he also continued to make spurs to order. I ordered probably ten pairs from him during my lifetime, and I ordered many for other people. I'd write down what a man wanted on his spurs and send the order to Ed. Of course, Ed knew these people, so he made the spurs and sent them to the man who ordered them, and the man would send him a check. He charged full price for those spurs, but he always gave me at least a 20 percent discount, just like he did a saddle shop. But I got no preferential treatment when it came to how fast he filled my order. He always put my order on the bottom like everyone else's. When it came to the top, he made my spurs. Once he had finished the work, he was always in a hurry to collect his money.

All through the years we tried to get Ed to charge more money for his spurs, because it was a break-even deal. In the early years, he spent four or five days making a pair of spurs and then charged only seven to ten dollars for them. He figured if he were working on a ranch for thirty or forty dollars a month and he could make two pairs of spurs a month in his spare time, he had an extra fifteen dollars. He was making more money than any other cowboy. He didn't care how many hours he worked. It was from "can see" until "can't see." There weren't many days off when a man worked on a ranch. It was usually seven days a week year round. Ed always had access to or owned a forge and anvil and a little steel—and a Harvey House fork and some copper and brass. That was how he worked in the early years. But Ed went at spur making in a more business-like manner once he was in Yucca.

Ed's brother Charlie went to El Paso every year to sign up for his old age pension. Ed usually took him or picked him up, and he would stop by to see us. About 1961 or 1962, he came by Water Canyon on his way to El Paso to get Charlie. He was driving a fairly new pickup, and he had a big sign on the door. Written in green letters was BLANCHARD SPURS, YUCCA, ARIZONA, and it had a picture of a spur.

"You're getting pretty modern there, Ed," I told him.

He looked down at the ground, sort of embarrassed. "Charles talked me into putting that on there. He said it would be a little advertising, but you know, it is pretty disgusting when you go through the country and someone stops you and asks what that sign means. It sure gets embarrassing sometimes."

His advertising must have helped. He told a journalist in 1962 that he turned out about 350 pairs of spurs a year.

Anytime Ed went to El Paso, he stopped by our home in Water Canyon and spent the night. For many years he would never sleep in the house. He always had his bedroll in the back of the pickup, and he just rolled it out and slept in his truck. I'd help him find a level spot, and that's where he'd sleep. Of course, he ate with us. As time went by and he got older, he rolled his bed out on our screened porch. He was always here in the fall or winter, so it was cold outside at night, but it didn't seem to bother him. Then the last few years that he came, during the 1970s, he had gotten pretty modern. He'd use the bathroom and sleep in the house.

He had a sister in Albuquerque, and I'd take him up there. He couldn't drive in the traffic. I don't know how he ever got to El Paso.

Ed Blanchard's shop was in a corrugated iron building behind his small house near Yucca, Arizona. Photo by Jane Pattie

I took him to Albuquerque one time and left him for three days and then went back and got him. Another time, I just took him for the day. He was always close to his family.

Ed and Charlie helped support their mother all her life. All of the kids gave money to their mother every month until she died. Then they supported their sister, Katherine, until she died. Ed would give you anything he had. Even though he was always nervous around. kids, he made spurs for all the kids. Some of the first spurs he ever made were for the Cook boys. And about 1932, he gave me the pair of kid's spurs that I still have. Most of the cowboys teased a kid, but Ed never did that. He would hardly talk to you. Maybe he just didn't know what to say. Paul Blanchard's daughter, Linda Whitaker of Clovis,

New Mexico, recalls Ed fondly as her favorite uncle. He gave her the first pair of boots she ever had.

Ed was peculiar about a lot of things, but he always paid his debts, and he expected to be paid what was due him. One time when he was in Water Canyon, I had to go to Socorro. Ed said he'd ride down there with me. We went into a cafe to drink coffee and let Ed visit with some of the old guys he had known thirty or forty years before. There were four or five men in there, and they all greeted Ed. He even grinned a little. They got to talking. There was one old guy who had been out around Datil in the 1930s and 1940s, and he kept trying to talk to Ed, but Ed just ignored him.

When we left, I asked Ed, "Didn't you know ol' Jack in there?"

"You bet I know Jack! In 1942, he ordered a pair of spurs from me, and he still owes me ten dollars. He's never gonna pay it, either!" Ed had a long memory.

On the way back to Water Canyon, we got to talking about his spurs and the people who had bought them. "You know, a funny thing happened," Ed said. "About two months ago, I had a letter from this nice feller way down in Texas. He wanted to order two pair of spurs and a pair of bits. You know what? I was just a little suspicious of this feller. He made me real itchy. I just sat down and wrote him a letter and asked him what he was gonna do with these spurs and bridle bits. In a while, I got an answer back. You'll never guess what he said. He said he wanted to hang them in his trophy room in his house. You know what I did? It didn't take me ten minutes to write him back and tell him that I did not make spurs and bridle bits to hang on the wall, and I was not making him any!"

Ed often said if he lived long enough to make spurs for everyone who wanted a pair, he'd die happy. He wanted the cowboys and cattlemen to have his spurs. He wasn't too interested in the city people owning them.

One year, Charlie took a Greyhound bus back to Yucca from El Paso. They were near Seligman when the bus ran off the highway, turned over on its side, and slid down the road for quite a way. Several people were hurt. Later, Charlie was telling Billy Cook about the accident. "You know, that sure was a wreck!" he said. "But I met the nicest feller there. This feller gathered us all together, and he gave us a card to sign. He said if we'd sign this card, he'd give us five dollars so we could eat supper." Of course, the card stated that no one would sue the company for the accident, but Charlie insisted, "He sure was a nice feller! I ate the best supper I've had in a long time."

Billy Cook just shook his head. It didn't do any good to explain the ways of the world to Charlie. He had his own way of looking at things.

Ed got religion while he was in Yucca. He would never say the words "whiskey" or "beer," even though he had swigged his share in his younger days. When he and Billy Cook were together, Billy would sometimes say, "Let's stop in here and get a drink."

"No," Ed would say. "I'm not going in there and watch you guys drink that stuff." He'd sul up. He never drank anything after he got religion. But I've seen him drink beer in Magdalena. If he was around Uncle Jim, he danged sure drank it!

I say he got religion after he went to Yucca, but he must have turned against drinking before that. Billy Cook recalls an incident that happened while the Cooks still owned the Currycomb Ranch. They had some cow work to do, and Ed had gone upriver to gather the horses and bring them down to headquarters. He didn't come in, and it was midafternoon before they saw him coming down the river with the horse herd. He rode up on the bank in front of the house and fell off his horse. The boys ran out to see what was wrong. Ed had passed out, and he was covered in big, red splotches.

Billy ran back to the house to get some whiskey to revive him. He came back with a pint bottle of Two Naturals that had about a drink left in the bottom. They poured it down Ed's throat. He sputtered and spewed, but it brought him around—and was he mad! "What do you mean pouring that stuff down me?" he said. He was really offended, but he was breathing again.

He had stopped at a windmill to get some water. He pushed his hat back on his head and leaned down to drink from the pipe. He didn't see the wasps around the pipe until they hit him. He was stung all over, and they almost killed him. It was a wonder he got back to house. I guess he would rather have died than drink that whiskey.

I don't know how he got religion, because for years he hated all preachers. He must have had a weak spell, and after that, everything was religion. Every letter he wrote to Hilda and me ended with "Think of the Lord" or "Pray to the Lord." And most of the money he made, he sent as donations to these television preachers.

Billy Cook told me that one time Ed sent one of these evangelists four hundred dollars. The man wrote him a letter back and told him to send six hundred dollars more. Ol' Ed was really nervous about this letter. He told Porter, "The preacher wrote me that if I didn't send the money, when I died, I'd be nowhere. I'd just be in orbit. What do you guess that means?"

Everything was a joke to Porter, and he liked to tease Ed. "I guess he meant you'd just be floating around somewhere," Porter said with a straight face.

Ed got pretty excited. "I don't have to worry about that." Ed was relieved to learn that he was going to heaven.

"You mean to tell me you sent that s.o.b. that six hundred dollars?" Porter exclaimed. "Ed Blanchard, I ought to just kill you myself!"

One thing about it—I guess Ed got out of orbit.

Ed still stayed worried about his religion. Porter Cook's eyes must have sparkled even though he kept a straight face the day he told Ed, "You know, Ed, you ought to become a preacher—you've been so honest all your life!"

One day he and Porter rode out to check cattle. They were sitting on their horses, looking out across the country, and Ed was making a big speech about the Lord. "I'm just trying to pay back for all the things I did when I was young," he said.

"What do you mean by that?" Porter asked.

Ed shook his head. "I did some bad things. I just hope I can live long enough to pay back for all the cows I stole."

Porter just grinned. "Ed, you'd have to live to be two hundred years old!"

Ol' Ed got mad and rode off.

In August, 1966, Hilda and I got a letter from Ed. He had had another weak spell. He said that he had a surprise for me. "I got married last Friday night in Las Vegas," he wrote. That *was* some surprise.

How he ever got to Las Vegas, Nevada, I'll never know. And whatever possessed him to get married when he was seventy-two years old, I'll never know. Anyway, he wrote that he had taken his new wife home with him.

That letter was the only time he ever mentioned her. We never knew anything about her except through our family connection with the Cooks.

This woman was about thirty-five or forty years old when she moved to Yucca with Ed and Charlie. Ed's little house had two bedrooms, and Ed used one and Charlie had the other. We were told that the new wife slept on the front porch. I guess that goes back to the Blanchard girls hanging their "under drawers" in the pillowcases.

I asked Billy Cook how long they stayed married, and he didn't know for sure. Aunt Mable visited Ed and Charlie one time, and Charlie was mad because this "damned, disgusting woman" was living there. Charlie would talk to Aunt Mable. "She's a sickening thing!" he said.

He told Aunt Mable he was taking a bath one day, and he was sitting in the tub. There was no lock on the bathroom door, and Ed's new wife busted right in. Charlie grabbed a towel to cover himself. The woman looked at him and said, "What's the matter with you? I don't think you've got anything I could see anyway."

"That was the most embarrassing moment of my whole life!" Charlie told Aunt Mable.

I guess the woman lasted a month or so before Ed sent her packing. After she had left, Ed told Aunt Mable that he had to buy her a new car and give her five thousand dollars. We never even knew her name, and he never mentioned her again in his letters. It was as though the marriage never happened.

Tally Cook died in 1958 after the family moved to Arizona. Mable eventually married a man named Jared Wooten. I only saw Jared one time, when he and Aunt Mable came to Water Canyon to visit. He was born in the 1880s, and he was from the Carlsbad area in southeastern New Mexico. He told me that he knew Pat Garrett and had talked with him on the road a short time before Pat was shot and killed.

While visiting in Water Canyon, Mable wanted to go to Socorro to see her longtime friends, Roby and Lilly Eiland. The Eilands originally came from Texas, but they had been in New Mexico since about 1925. Hilda and I went with Mable and Jared.

Frank Kelly and his son Tom at the old Kelly place in Water Canyon in 1953. Frank holds Tom and Hilda's daughter, Kim. Courtesy Tom Kelly

Mable introduced Jared to Roby and Lilly. Jared and Roby seemed to really hit it off, and they talked about horses, cows, and ranching for about thirty minutes. Out of the clear blue, Jared said to Roby, "Well, kid, did you ever learn to ride a bronc any better than you could when you were fifteen?"

Roby looked rather surprised, but they started talking about old times. By then I figured out they had known one another years before. Later I asked Roby, "Didn't you recognize ol' Jared when you saw him?"

"Hell, yes!" he said. "That was the meanest man I ever knew!" It turned out that years before when Roby was a big kid, Jared was trying to teach him to ride broncs, but Roby kept getting thrown, so he hung onto the saddle horn. Jared would ride along beside him and beat his hands off of the horn with the top end of his quirt, which was made of a piece of iron about six inches long and covered with braided leather. Several broncs later when evening came, Roby said his hands were pretty bloody.

Ed Blanchard in his shop near Yucca, Arizona, in 1973. Photo by Jane Pattie

The next morning he rode better, since his hands were so swollen he couldn't touch the saddle horn. Jared still rode alongside him just in case. Some of those old cowboys were a little different.

Needless to say, Mable and Jared's marriage didn't last. They were separated and had been for a while when Mable died in 1968.

Ed was always behind on his spur orders even before he hit Yucca. Every time he came to Water Canyon to visit he'd say, "I'm two months behind on my spurs. I just hope I live long enough to get them all made." One time he told me he was making sixteen pairs a week. I've often wondered how many he made during the years he had his Arizona shop, but it must have been a bunch. The majority were made there in Yucca after 1959 and before he had his stroke.

Charlie died April 17, 1970. Ed's health became bad in the late 1970s, and he had a debilitating stroke. He spent his last few years in a nursing home in Kingman. That must have been hard on a man who was use to sleeping in his bedroll with the brilliant stars overhead—and drinking thick, black coffee that would melt a tin cup—and cinching his saddle on tough broncs—or riding hell-bent down Baldy's canyons chasing an ol' wild cow. Perhaps what he missed the most was the ring of his hammer as he beat out a spur on his anvil.

"I just hope I live long enough to make spurs for every cowboy who wants a pair," Ed once said. That didn't happen. Edward Fred Blanchard died January 17, 1982.

Ed Blanchard made spurs to be used by horsemen and cowmen, and they can still be found jingling on many a cowboy's boot heels. However, they have also taken their rightful places in museums and private collections across the country. If Ed knew that, he would snort and say, "Now that's just damned sickening! I didn't make spurs to hang on a wall! I made them for cowboys to use."

Ranching in Blanchard Country Then and Now

by Tom Kelly

The people who populated the Magdalena country of New Mexico, where Ed Blanchard and I grew up and where I still live, were in the most part ranchers, sheepmen, mining men, prospectors, and of course, the merchants, who supplied everything they all needed. The Santa Fe Railway made life easier in 1885, when it completed a line between Socorro and Magdalena to haul goods and passengers as well as ore and stock. The railroad operated from 1885 until 1971 and was a lifeline to all the people of the area. However, it was ranching that influenced my life and Ed Blanchard's life the most.

During the 1870s and 1880s, if a man had a few cows and a couple of horses, he could become a rancher. He first had to find a spring of water, dig it out, and build a log house or rock shack and a small corral, and then he changed from cowboy to cowman. To stay in business, he kept up a running fight with the mountain lions, bears, wolves, coyotes, and everything and everyone else who was hungry. There were no fences, so the rancher herded his livestock during the day and shut them up at night in the corral next to the house. The cows stayed in or near the mountains, since there was no water out on the flats.

If a man needed more cattle, he could likely find a neighbor who did not take care of his animals. He kind of "borrowed" a few of the neighbor's unbranded calves or yearlings and put his own brand on them. Now if he liked his neighbor and they got along, he didn't do this. This neighbor might have a few extras that came from farther north, and the rancher had some show up accidentally from down south, so they might make a trade. Once in a while, either one might borrow a fat yearling from the other to eat just as a joke to see if the other was staying on his toes. If the rancher had a neighbor that no one especially liked, he'd let him steal a cow just to prove the man was a thief. Then the rancher felt justified in stealing three or four of the neighbor's cows to replace the one he had stolen. Before he did that, he made sure he had more nerve and was a better cowboy than his neighbor was.

One old-timer might be eating dinner with another. The first one says, "John, how do you like that steak?"

John, to be polite, says, "Sure is mighty tasty."

"Well, John, it was one of yours. Don't you recognize it?"

"It sure could be," John says. "Come to think of it, I never ate one of my own before!"

Neither one would ever know for sure who was telling the truth, but probably both were.

It wasn't long before eastern people came to the country, as they had in Texas. They bought up water holes or just claimed them and turned thousands of cattle loose on the open range. These cattle scattered all over the country for miles, and of course, the newcomers didn't or couldn't take care of them. The rancher who was already here with the few cows, a log shack, and two horses had a head start. Soon, more and more of the easterner's cows drank the rancher's water and ate the grass since the land was not fenced. Before long, there was not enough grass or water for the rancher's cows, so the ranchers who were here to begin with started thinning out the easterner's herd. The easterner couldn't figure out why he couldn't make money in the cattle business, and he soon went back where he came from. Of course, his cattle stayed in New Mexico with new brands on them.

As time went by, these first cowboys bought the water rights from the government by using forty-acre land scrip. This made each of them the proud owner of forty acres, probably little more than a pile of rocks. He still ran his cattle on open range. He worked himself to death every day, half starved, and had no money, but he got by.

The old-time cowboy was completely different from today's cowboy. He didn't own much—a horse, a worn-out saddle (which usually ate big holes in his horse's back if he rode the same horse every day), pants, shirt, and sometimes socks. He had boots that never fit or a pair of lace boots that he wore half-laced. He owned a coat of some kind, a knife, usually a gun, spurs, a rope, and a bedroll. He also had a hat and long-handle underwear, which he never took off. If he had a pretty steady job, he probably had a second set of clothes that he used for dress-up in case he went to town. If not, he bought new clothes when he got there.

He generally stayed on the ranch where he worked for six months to a year before he got to town. When he went to town, he usually had all of his pay in his pocket—maybe $150 to $300. The first things he did were to get a room and have a haircut and bath. He stopped at the general store to buy new clothes, a hat, and boots. Then he went to the bar to catch up on the news. He enjoyed a little whiskey and a poker game that lasted until he spent all his money. Of all the gamblers who used to be in town and all the money the cowboys lost to them playing poker, few of the gamblers had a nickel to their names when they died. They were just as broke as the cowboys.

Most cowboys had this terrible good time when they got to town even though they were usually without a job since it was the fall of the year. Ranchers cut back on their hired help after they shipped their cattle. So the next morning, there the cowboy was, standing on the corner by Becker-Mactavish General Store or in front of the bar. He had no money in the pocket of his new clothes and was out of a job. He probably felt a little sick from too much firewater.

He did not appear worried, however. He'd ride the chuck line all winter and go from ranch to ranch. He would work a little for a bed and grub until spring when he could get a job again. He usually didn't last long at any one place during the winter. All the rancher had to do to make him move on was to tell him to chop a little wood or milk the cow. Or the rancher would fail to keep a night horse up and tell the cowboy to go wrangle the horses on foot. If the rancher wanted him gone in a hurry, he'd have his wife suggest that the cowboy pack a little water so he could help wash clothes. She might even get the old No. 3 washtub down and suggest he take a bath. He would leave in a hurry, probably muttering to himself, "G__-damned woman-run outfit! Who could stay around here! I'm a cowboy, not a damn milk maid or cleaning woman! And by G__, cowboys don't walk, either! They ride! I walk from the house to the corral and to the outhouse, and by G__ that's enough! And take a bath in winter—G__! What are things comin' to? A man could catch cold and die!"

Put this same cowboy to work at what he thought he was supposed to do, and he generally did a good job. He had a forty- to sixty-foot rope and could use it. He could catch anything, anywhere, anytime. He didn't care if it was in the brush or on the steepest, rockiest hill. He tied his rope onto his saddle, and it stayed there until he needed it. After all, it cost a couple of dollars.

In his opinion, a horse wasn't any good unless it had a little life in it. It could buck four times a day and try to kill him every time, but the cowboy thought it was "the best damn horse ever born."

The cattleman who owned the ranch and the cattle had to be a little smarter and work longer than the general run of cowboy, or maybe his head was harder. He came to be the proud owner of this piece of real estate by being there first, being meaner, and working harder than anyone else. He might also have won the land in a poker game or stolen it from someone else.

If he had a wife, it helped, because being married made him stay home and take care of things. As any kind of woman was hard to find in this country, he was kind of lucky. She could always cook and chop wood if the ax was sharp when she started. She could milk the cow, but if she got kicked, it was her fault. It was her job to take care of the grubby, snotty-nosed kids with the patched clothes and worn-out shoes. She could ride a horse if she had to and work cows a little, if she didn't get lost first. No matter where she was, she was always in the wrong place and always turned the cow the wrong direction. The horse she rode was either lazy or kept running off into the trees. To make matters worse, when they went to town, she couldn't even go into the bar, so it was best to leave her home!

The poor wife probably thought the rancher was a hard-headed ol' s.o.b. and told him so. He never made enough money, and he spent what they did have on bulls and horses. He never helped with the dishes or took the ashes out of the stove. He didn't fix the leaks in the roof, and the nails in the heels of his boots made holes in the floor. He never helped with the kids, and he taught them to cuss. He was gone nearly all the time, and when he was home, he stayed mad most of the time. When he did take the family to town, he drove as if he were riding a horse—down the middle of the road or on the wrong side while he looked around. When they finally got to town, he spent all his time in the bar. There didn't seem to be much difference between a rancher and a cowboy.

The rancher had the cattle and the ranch that he, the wife, and banker owned together. His brand was on the cattle, so he got to worry with them and brag on them, but every fall, the banker got all the money when they were sold. Then the banker lent it back to the rancher a little at a time, knowing he would get it back the next fall.

Every once in a while, the banker would want to count the rancher's cattle to see if he had as many as he had mortgaged. If the rancher was short fifty head when the banker came to count, he would round some of them up and run them past the banker again, who then left satisfied. To satisfy the banker the next year, he'd also have to 'count' more cattle that he didn't have. That could go on forever. He then had three choices: change bankers and start over; go broke, which he already was; or sell most of the cows to pay off the bank.

Every once in a while, the rancher had a good year. The price of cows would go up. The banker would be a little friendlier and even smile while the rancher signed the note for next year's loan. To the rancher, "next year" was always going to be better.

At first, ranchers from the Magdalena area shipped their cattle by rail to Kansas City to be sold. They were usually three- or four-year-old steers that brought four to eight dollars per head in Kansas City. The Santa Fe Railway gave the owner a free round-trip ticket to Kansas City to sell his cattle.

Then came the cow buyer, who usually bought them in Magdalena, and he shipped them. The cow buyer came every year at least once.

He was a lot jollier than the banker. He liked to talk a lot, drink a lot, eat a lot, gamble, and chase the girls. He stayed in the hotel, and he took several baths a year, so he smelled better than the cowboy. He was the one who lost money on the rancher's cattle last year. "They've gone down this year," he would lament. "Bad market." If the cattle were fat, he wanted them poor; if they were poor, he wanted them fat.

He wore a good suit of clothes and had a big gold watch with a gold chain across his whey belly. He wore a 10X beaver hat and probably drove a fancy Model T Ford. He probably had a gold ring or two on his fingers and a gold tie clasp, but he'd tell the rancher he'd have to buy his cattle cheaper than last year to break even. He had a pen or pencil to figure with, but he just scraped off a smooth spot in the dirt and figured out what the cowman had coming.

The rancher always thought it rained first and more on his neighbor's place than on his. He wasn't sure why that was, so he would sometimes sneak a little money to the preacher. Maybe the neighbor had quit stealing cows or he had been a little kind-hearted to his wife. Whatever it was, God was sure favoring him.

The cowman knew the country for miles around. He had been over it many times horseback. He knew every rock, ditch, hill, and tree. He could get around about as good in the dark as in the daytime. He knew his cows by sight and could probably tell you which bull sired each calf and when it was born. Most of them had names. He rode every day all day long. He knew which cow would be on a certain hill or in which canyon, because she always ran there.

He could remember things from years past. "See that rock over there across the canyon? Well, George and I were sitting right here on October 22, 1914. When a big ol' black bear came around that rock, we shot him. Yep . . . he sure was fat!"

A rancher didn't have much use for a pen and paper. He didn't write anything down. And he didn't get much mail—no junk mail, no government forms, no bad checks, and very little money to count. When he made a deal to sell his cattle, there was no contract—just his word and that of the buyer and the date. The buyer's money was good, and the rancher's word was good, so there was no need to write it down.

The rancher bought almost everything he and his family needed at a general store in Magdalena—groceries, clothing, boots, hats, cosmetics, kitchen and household goods, building supplies, rope, saddles, guns, well supplies, salt, grain, alfalfa, anything. They had it. There were several stores in town. If a rancher didn't borrow money for expenses from the bank, he had credit at the store. He paid his bill once a year in the fall when he sold his cattle. It was usually six hundred to eight hundred dollars yearly, depending on how big his operation was. If the rancher was a good customer, when he paid his bill, Bill Dobson, who ran Macdonald Company, usually gave him a carton of Prince Albert or Bull Durham smoking tobacco. The wife and kids got a box of candy. At the Becker-Mactavish store, he might get a nip out of Mr. Mactavish's special bottle of hooch that he kept behind the counter.

Sometimes after the rancher paid off his loan, if he had a little left, he deposited it at the store so he could draw on it when needed. The merchant did not pay interest on this money, and the rancher did not pay interest on his yearly grocery bill, either. In those days, the merchant and the rancher trusted each other. The store owner made very little profit on each item but managed to stay in business.

The first cattle in the Magdalena country were out of milk pen stock. They were every color, size, and kind. Before the railroad and during the early days, cattle were traded and sold and slaughtered locally. The butcher shop cut them up and sold a steak at a time to their customers. The railroad reached Socorro in 1880. Soon after, eastern moneyed men began buying land and shipping cattle to the area. They thought they were going to make a killing. In 1884, the Santa Fe Railway began laying a track west from Socorro and reached Magdalena in January, 1885. It brought more people, more business, and more cattle to the area.

The V+T Ranch, owned by the Red River Land and Cattle Company, was one of these new outfits. The Duke's Mixture Tobacco Company owned most or all of the V+T operation. They bought some water rights and claimed a lot of country. They had thousands of cattle scattered from the Rio Grande to the Arizona state line. They brought the first Hereford bulls into the country. Everyone soon had some of their bulls. If they didn't, they made a point to borrow a few, because they were better cattle than they had. The cattle in the area were upgraded by these Herefords. The local ranchers figured that if they smoked the company's tobacco, why couldn't they use the company's bulls and eat its beef?

The old-timers who carried long ropes eventually killed the goose that laid the golden egg. The V+T went broke or just sold out and left. Of course, many of their cattle and their offspring stayed, with someone else's brand on them. Then the rancher had to go out and buy his bulls somewhere else. Cow buyers wanted good cattle, and the better they were, the more they would pay. By the 1930s, everyone had most of the milk-cow look bred out of the herds. The buyers were getting so particular, they wouldn't take a cow that was red-eyed, line-backed, or bob-tailed. They cut them out and would not buy them.

By the 1940s, about the only cattle sold were yearlings. There wasn't much market for old cows or calves. In those days, the country supported five to ten times as many cattle as it does now. Since it snowed every winter, there was plenty of green grass in the spring until June, when things dried up. The rains came again the first of July and the grass grew all summer, but the country was soon overstocked. When a dry year came along, thousands of cattle died. There was no market for them. Owners could not sell them and they couldn't feed them, so the cattle died. The rancher ended up with half the cattle he had had, but it gave the country a chance to come back.

In a few years, everything looked good again. The banker smiled, the wife didn't talk about the leaky roof so often, and the kids had new patches on their pants. It looked like the rancher would make it if he didn't have any more dry years for a while, if he didn't go to town very often, if he could keep borrowing money, if no more cows died, and if the wife stayed with him.

Now those tough old-timers are gone. If a rancher thinks or acts like one, people think he's a damn fool or was born fifty years too late. Everyone has become educated smart and everything is modern. Now no one has to worry about the outhouse blowing over or whether or not there are enough Montgomery Ward catalogs to last all year. Ranchers really have it made!

The cow buyer still comes. He still says he lost money on the rancher's cows last year. The cows are still too fat or too poor. The cow buyer still has the 10X beaver hat. The big gold watch and chain have been replaced by a wristwatch that tells him the time, date, and month so he won't miss his next appointment. He still has a whey belly, but diamond rings now replace the gold rings. The big Cadillac that has replaced the Model T drags all the high spots and rocks out of the middle of your dirt road. The cow buyer still arrives just in time to eat, and he eats as much as always. He smells better than the buyer of years past because he probably stayed in a high-dollar motel room where he had a bath before coming to your place. His pen or pencil is gone, and there's no more figuring in the dirt to see how much he owes you. He uses a pocket calculator that makes mistakes and you don't trust, but his checks are still good.

The rancher now must have a lawyer to advise him, an accountant to keep his books, and the government to tell him how many cows he has and how to manage his operation. Of course, the government made him get a Social Security number, so it could keep track of him. And then every year he must give the government part of his income, if there is any. All of this is for his benefit so that when he gets old, he can retire and live like a king on three hundred dollars a month.

The ranch's rock shack or log house is gone, replaced by a fancy house built by an absentee owner. The spring of water has dried up. The land that cost five hundred dollars eighty years ago costs two million now. The money made off of the cattle running there will barely pay for taking care of them. The price paid for the land and cattle makes wonderful deductions on the owner's taxes. There are still a lot of horses ridden and cows chased by the modern cowboy, but most of it is done while sitting on a bar stool or drinking coffee in the cafe.

The rancher now sends his kids to college to learn to be smart so they can be cowboys. The good Hereford cattle that the old-timers bragged about that took years to breed up so they populated the country are gone. In those days, a rancher got a good calf crop out of them, in some cases 90 to 95 percent every year, and everybody wanted them. Now the ranchers have gone to what they call "crossbreds." Almost everyone thinks they are great. They look just like the ones that were here in 1890. Their color is the same; they get just as wild; most of them have a calf every other year like they used to; no one has to buy any good bulls to breed the cows to, because good, bad, or whatever, they all look about the same. They sell good, because almost everyone thinks they're great.

A large part of the cattle are what they call calves, shipped from Texas, Florida, Mexico, or someplace else to summer in New Mexico by these absentee landowners who own many of the ranches now. "Yep," the owner will say. "Just calves—325 pounds—came clear from Mexico. Little buggers are sure gonna do good this summer!"

If "Ol' Yep" would look at their teeth when he brands them, he would learn that most of them are two- or three-year-olds. He'll probably put three times as many on the land as he should. They will starve a little, just as they have done all their lives. If he is lucky, he'll put a hundred pounds on them. What survives after shipping fever, half starving, and poor care will probably only lose fifty to one hundred dollars per head. But it will do wonders for the owner's income tax deduction, which he really needs because his oil wells or other enterprises are killing him tax-wise.

The old-time cowman spent years getting rid of the wolves, lions, bears, and coyotes. He made it safe for livestock and people to live here. By 1920, he had predators pretty well cut down, and he was losing very few cattle to them. The deer herds had built back to where there were plenty of deer for the predators to eat as nature intended, so they didn't bother the cattle. New Mexico established its game department about this time, and they continued this type of management.

Then all of the sudden things changed. The people running the government organizations had a new viewpoint. They began saving the coyote and the lion. They did such a good job that the predators have eaten most of the deer and therefore, they are hungry. Now the rancher's cattle are beginning to feed the lions and coyotes again as they did in 1900.

Yes, the rancher now has it made. The environmentalists, the scientists, the accountants, and all the other government bureaucrats control the rancher's land, cattle, money, and life. It looks as though the old-time cowman was lucky that he missed all these good times.

Today's cowman still stays on the ranch, saddles his horse almost every day, and knows where his cattle are. You can usually tell a cowman by sight because when he walks through the corral, he doesn't hop around trying to miss the piles of fresh cow manure. He wades right through it, and when he gets to the house, he still catches hell from his wife for what he does to the carpet. He still goes to town for supplies, but he has to drive on his side of the road because he doesn't have the road to himself anymore. There are a hundred other fools just like him headed for town, but the cowman still survives.

In spite of all the changes, if ol' Ed could once more ride along Water Canyon up to the Kellys' camp on Mount Baldy and urge his horse into a ground-eating lope with a touch from his Blanchard spurs, he'd know he was home.

BIBLIOGRAPHY

BOOKS AND ARTICLES

Ball, Eve. *In the Days of Victorio: Recollections of a Warm Springs Apache.*
    Tucson: University of Arizona Press, 1970.
Beck, Warren A. *New Mexico—A History of Four Centuries.* Norman: Univer-
    sity of Oklahoma Press, 1962.
Bryan, Howard. *Wildest of the Wild West.* Santa Fe, N.Mex.: Clear Light
    Publishers, 1991.
Callon, Milton. "The Carlos Blanchard Chronicle." *Frontier Times,* October–
    November, 1967.
———. *Las Vegas, New Mexico—The Town That Wouldn't Gamble.* Las Vegas,
    N.Mex.: Las Vegas Daily Optic, Las Vegas Publishing Company, 1962.
Celebrating 100 Years of Frontier Living. Magdalena, N.Mex.: Magdalena Old
    Timers Association, 1994.
Chilton, Lance, et al. *New Mexico: A New Guide to a Colorful State.* Albuquer-
    que: University of New Mexico Press, 1984.
Connor, Seymour V., and Jimmy M. Skaggs. *Broadcloth and Britches: The
    Santa Fe Trade.* College Station: Texas A&M University Press, 1977.
Davis, Ellis Arthur, ed. *The Historical Encyclopedia of New Mexico.* Vol. 2.
    Albuquerque: New Mexico Historical Association, 1945.
French, Capt. William. *Some Recollections of a Western Ranchman, New Mexico,
    1883–1899.* New York: Frederick A. Stokes, 1928. Reprint, Silver City,
    N.Mex.: High-Lonesome Books, 1997.
Gnatkowski, Mel. "Blanchards." *Arizona Rancher,* September–October,
    1994, 26–28.
Haley, J. Evetts. *Charles Goodnight—Cowman and Plainsman.* Norman:
    University of Oklahoma Press, 1949.
Horgan, Paul. *Great River: The Rio Grande in North American History.* New
    York: Rinehart and Company, 1954.
Ormes, Robert M. *Guide to the Colorado Mountains.* Denver: Sage Books,
    1952.
Pattie, Jane. *Cowboy Spurs and Their Makers.* College Station: Texas A&M
    University Press, 1991.
Perrigo, Lynn. *Gateway to Glorieta: A History of Las Vegas, New Mexico.*
    Boulder, Colo.: Pruett Publishing Company, 1982.
Sprague, Marshall. *Colorado: A Bicentennial History.* New York: Norton,
    1976.

Trimble, Marshall. A*rizona: A Panoramic History of a Frontier State.* Garden City, N.Y.: Doubleday, 1977.

CORRESPONDENCE

Letters from E. F. Blanchard, Yucca, Ariz., to Tom Kelly. Tom Kelly Collection, Water Canyon, N.Mex.:
Nov. 12, 1965
Aug. 17, 1966
Apr. 23, 1967
Aug. 28, 1967
July 6, 1969
July 28, 1974
Oct. 14, 1975
Discounted invoice for spurs dated Sept. 25, 1969. Tom Kelly Collection, Water Canyon, N.Mex.

INDEX